ACROSS SCOTLAND ON FOOT

A Guide for Walkers and Hill Runners

to David Howard for the walks
to Glyn Jones for the runs
to Clare for the coming home afterwards

ACROSS SCOTLAND ON FOOT

A Guide for Walkers and Hill Runners

By Ronald Turnbull

Grey Stone Books

Hoddlesden

First published in 1994 by
Grey Stone Books

British Library Cataloguing in Publication Data

A catalogue record of this book is available from the British Library.

ISBN 0 9515996-4-X

Acknowledgments
I would like to thank all those who have helped me with the production of this book. Thanks to David Howard for the walks, to Glyn Jones for the runs, and to Clare for the coming home afterwards. Jean Robson kindly looked over Chapter 8, finding it hard to reconcile her caution as a doctor with her enthusiasm as a fell runner. The chapter would have been less sane and responsible without her. One of my vices as a runner is not carrying a camera in case it slows me down. Fortunately Jim Teesdale, Jeremy Ashcroft Irvine Butterfield, David Howard, Peter Pritchard, Andy Priestman and Phil Iddon have taken some of the photos I didn't - doubly fortunate as theirs are much better than mine would have been. The maps were drawn by me, the sketches are by John Gillham.

Ronald Turnbull was born in St Andrews (on the East Coast!) in 1951 into a mountaineering family. His grandfather was president of the Scottish Mountaineering Club. A great-uncle was killed in the Devil's Kitchen.

He climbed his first Munro, Glas Maol, at the age of nine and has since climbed on the Eiger, Mont Blanc and Kilimanjaro. He has crossed Scotland from one coast to the other five times in boots and twice in running shoes. In 1992 he ran the Bob Graham Round in 22½ hours and is the current record-holder of the Gallow Way. He was part-editor of the SMC's Guide to the West Highlands (Vol 3); exploration for this work involved him in two First Ascents and one of these (Thin Man's Ridge on Beinn Eighe: Severe) earned a place in the current edition of the guide. He also enjoys skiing without being any good at it, and once came last in a triathlon.

Ronald lives in Dumfriesshire with his wife, the illustrator Clare Melinsky and two children. As well as the SMC, he has written for Strider, Scottish Hill Runner, The Great Outdoors, Trail Walker and the Sanquhar Pantomime. He is the organiser of the Durisdeer Hill Race.

Front Cover: Creagan Coire Etchachan from Coire Etchachan beneath Ben Macdui in the Cairngorms (see Chapter Two). Photo by Jeremy Ashcroft
Rear Cover photo: The western coast at Lochranza, Isle of Arran by John Gillham

CONTENTS

Introduction   7

1   Convenient Coast to Coast   11
     Evanton to Poolewe

2   The Two Tops   23
     Stonehaven to Portree

3   Summits of the South   57
     Oban to Arbroath

4   Rough Galloway   84
     Gatehouse of Fleet to Girvan

5   The Southern Upland Way or Not   95
     Cocksburnpath to Portpatrick

6   The Wide Way in a Week   107
     Ardnamurchan Point to Peterhead

7   Absurdly Romantic Mull   113
     Iona to Craignure

8   Style and Accommodation   125

9   Luggage   128

10   Food   130

11   Planning   137

12   Reference   147

THE ROUTES

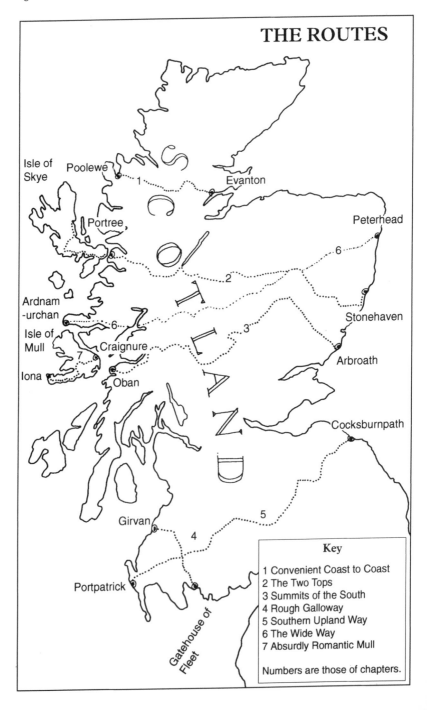

Isle of Skye
Poolewe
Evanton
Portree
Peterhead
Ardnam-urchan
Stonehaven
Isle of Mull
Craignure
Arbroath
Iona
Oban
Cocksburnpath
Girvan
Portpatrick
Gatehouse of Fleet

1
2
3
6
6
7
5
4

Key

1 Convenient Coast to Coast
2 The Two Tops
3 Summits of the South
4 Rough Galloway
5 Southern Upland Way
6 The Wide Way
7 Absurdly Romantic Mull

Numbers are those of chapters.

Introduction

Scotland is just the right size. The 277 Munros are a project of just the right length for a lifetime. Walking or running from one sea to another is always a challenge, yet one that nobody in reasonable health need fear.

In recent years we've realised that you do not have to be a skinny male with piercing aristocratic eyes and a resting pulse rate of twenty-seven to run the Marathon and in fact anyone who really wants to do it can.

Crossing Scotland is easier than running 26.2 miles along a road. It's also a whole lot more fun. You can take the high road, chaining together ridges and plateaux in an intensive geography experience. This was the way the pioneers - of Robertson, Naismith and Sir Hugh Munro himself, and it's still a very good way. Or you can take the low road, finding out the wild and narrow passes between one piece of country and the next as humans have been doing since before we became humans. Either way, you'll breathe the clean heather air of dawn; you'll see the cloud suddenly rise and the sunlight in wet corries; you'll cross a ridge and find half of Scotland before you; you'll descend at evening to remote bothies or arrive, soaked through, at hospitable Highland inns with a fire in the bar. You will come to know Scotland with your feet and find it smaller.

This book offers 108 ways to cross Scotland. Four of the routes are described in guide book detail: The Convenient Coast to Coast, the Two Tops, and Rough Galloway and a crossing of Mull. The Southern Upland Way has its own good waymarks, maps and guidebooks. Four other crossings are given in outline only; you can trace out our routes on the map but my hope here is not that you will follow our footprints through the bog but learn from our mistakes and build on our successes. The other hundred routes are in the four final chapters on how to devise your own. Many happy hours can be spent walking the glens of Scotland across the 1:50000 map, while the Autumn rains beat on the slates.

Two notes apply to the whole book. Some authorities add 20% to measured distances. I don't: I measure distances with a map measurer and I don't add anything for wiggles or distance up slopes. As a result, you will find my miles rather long ones. Horizontal distances will be given along with vertical feet of climb, which is often more important: 1000 feet of climb is as tiring as two extra miles. When I say "track" I mean something without tarmac but which has been or could be used by Landrovers. When I say "path" I mean something for people, for sheep, but not for things with wheels.

It was in 1972 that I set out with my friend David to cross Scotland - it was to take us seventeen years to get to the other side. We didn't take the tent - a fine robust tent it was, with wooden poles and thick canvas walls. We'd carried that tent up Glen Affric the summer before and we

Cairn Toul, looking down the SE ridge. (The long, long boulderslope out of Lairig Ghru. Photo: Jeremy Ashcroft

didn't want to carry it anywhere else, ever. Instead our stout canvas off-the-shoulder rucksacks were stuffed with warm woolly jumpers, cheese sandwiches, hand-mixed muesli and two large orange plastic bags.

The idea of the orange bag was a simple one. You woke up miserable but alive. However, provided you stayed on top of the thing and didn't actually get inside it you could stay fairly dry - just so long as it didn't rain. But if you slept inside it, you woke up with a sleeping bag that took four days to dry out. When you'd slept once inside the orange bag you walked the rest of the day and then went home.

Our route was not imaginative but it was long. From Glen Clova by Jock's Road to Braemar: then by Glen Feshie and the Corrieyairack to the Great Glen and northwards by Glen Affric and the Falls of Glomach to Torridon. We thought it would take us three or four days. But David started with an upset stomach, and as I enjoyed the views of the Lochnagar plateau he was looking no further than the next tuft of heather to crouch behind.

That was an interesting experience in tentless travel, but one that came to an end at the A9. For a while after that we neglected hillwalking in favour of Real Life. We took up smoking, paid employment and other vices. Then David wrote to say that he'd just done the Wainwright and that the Southern Upland Way passed three miles north of my house and what was I going to do about it? One thing, recounted in Chapter 5, led to another, recounted in Chapter 2.

If a Thing's Worth Doing It's Worth Doing Fast

"As we sat on the ridge enjoying the view and a well-earned cigar a pair of fell runners came panting and sweating up the screes. What can we say of these people who turn the temples of Nature into a racetrack, and do so moreover in tights?"

The result of this kind of remark is that when we runners pass you we put on fixed grins of enjoyment and gaze in an interested way at the horizon. We tend to speed up a bit too - our vanity doesn't just extend to the tights.

Many members of the Long Distance Walkers' Association now wear trainers, travel light and jog over the dull bits; and prejudiced remarks about bumbags are getting less common. In fact each route has its own appointed speed. For the Convenient Coast-to-Coast (Chapter 1) this is a slow amble with frequent stops to enjoy the scenery and if necessary to paint it in watercolours. For the Southern Upland Way, briefly covered in Chapter 5, a brisk run is best over the ever-lengthening forest roads. There is as much difference among those who enjoy the hills with different sizes of leg-muscles as there is among those who enjoy a concert with different sizes of ears.

Nevertheless, if I were not a runner I wouldn't have been on the Carn Mor Dearg Arete at dawn with cloud filling the valleys below right to the horizon. I wouldn't have crossed the Kilpatrick bogs alone in October by moonlight. If you want to become a runner, you will find in this book some discreet encouragement. If you don't, I hope to tempt you into other forms of imaginative eccentricity: perhaps the starlit bivouac (Chapter 8), or the crossing skis (Chapter 12). Or quite simply, at whatever pace suits you best, to make your way on foot from one coast of Scotland to the other.

Looking down over the Loch Valley from the granite slabs of Craignaw, a rugged scene so typical of the Galloway Hills, visited in Chapter 4.   *Photo: Andy Priestman*

Chapter One

THE CONVENIENT COAST to COAST

Evanton to Poolewe

Every year hundreds of people cross Scotland coast to coast: two hundred and fifty of them as part of the Great Outdoor Challenge (formerly the Ultimate Challenge) alone. As you go you fantasise about the perfect coast to coast: the one that includes the Mamores Ridge but where Rannoch Moor takes just three hours; the one where you compress the whole of the Eastern Grampians into a single flat-topped hill so as to climb them all at once; the one where the road section between the hills and the sea takes just twenty minutes. Then you would like the Carn Mor Dearg Arete and perhaps a little bit of Aonach Eagach: a stretch of Glen Feshie and of course a selection of the Wonderful West. Then again it would be nice to have bothies all the way and do without a tent ....

This dream crossing exists - it runs across the far north from Evanton to Poolewe. It is the Convenient Coast-to-Coast.

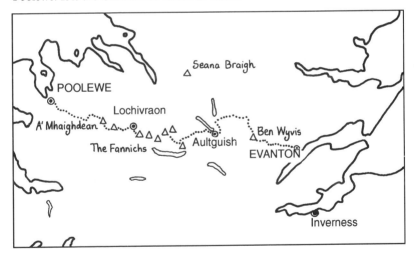

DAY 0
Evanton to Evanton
Distance 3 Miles

The dreary road bit between the sea and the hills can be dealt with in running shoes the evening before you set off on the main trek. Leave the main street beside the church and cross above the railway and the A9. The road becomes a farm track and then a path through woods on the north bank of the River

Sgitheach. If I had seen the path on the old Second Series O.S. map I would have gone half a mile up the shore to establish my walk start at the Balconie Point trig pillar, which may be the lowest in Scotland at four metres above mean sea level. Return by the same route.

DAY 1
Evanton to Aultguish
Ben Wyvis, Abhainn Beinn nan Eun, Strathvaich
Distance   28 miles
Ascent   5100 feet

We made a way out of the back of the camp site, which wasn't right but if we had taken the track that meets the main street immediately south of the camp site we wouldn't have met the badger. The badger was off to work or he would have stopped and raised a paw in greeting: the rest of them still asleep but we know when the world's at its best, you and I.

Black Rock Gorge is a splendid sandstone slit - deep, dripping and slimy. Don't approach it if you've a poor head for heights or deep-seated Freudian insecurities. The two bridges across it are quite unsuitable for playing pooh-sticks as any twigs you drop are lost in the gloom long before they hit the water. The bridges are also closer together than the map realises. (We took the second to be a new one and continued up the south bank by a gradually vanishing path through woods with invisible waters roaring far below. Eventually the path escaped into obscurity and we broke our way out to the Drumore Farm track at GR 583663. The paths that continue from this track into the forest do, surprisingly, exist.) The simpler way is to cross the bridge to the north bank, then take the road and track by Redburn.

The two tracks around the Cnoc a Mhargadaidh provide an unusual dilemma. They are the same in every respect and there is no rational way to choose between them. One could cut the Gordian Cnoc by going straight over the top but this is not recommended. (Apologies to English readers: Cnoc is a knob-shaped hill. Gordian knot: confronted with this puzzler tied by King Gordius, Alexandra the Great unsportingly took out his sword and slashed the ropes. It's a machete you would need on the Mhargadaidh.)

The Landrover track onto the moor goes further west than the new map (sheet 20) suggests and then the grassy banks of the Allt nan Caorach slip you through the heather. We bashed the shrubbery up Leacann Bhreac and round nicely enough to Tom a Choinnich but when I go back I'll apply my own rule for going up hills: *go right into the corrie with the lochan in it.*

I'll stay with the stream to the foot of Loch a Choire Mhoir, then turn uphill (west) after the first crags but before the waterfall. Above the waterfall turn south alongside the stream that feeds it. Steep, grassy slopes lead onto the shoulder known as An Socach. This route isn't just the map's idea. I worked it out from the other side of the corrie.

There have been one or two moments on the way up when the pleasure could almost be taken for work, but the stroll across short grass and old snow to Wyvis summit is positively Sunday-after-lunch stuff. If it is clear and

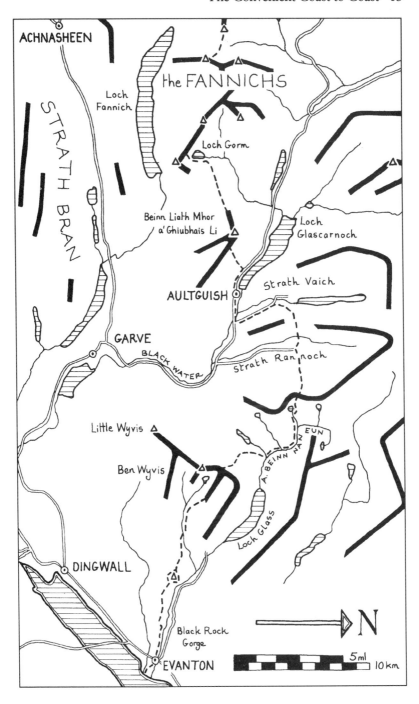

ACHNASHEEN

the FANNICHS

Loch Fannich

STRATH BRAN

Loch Gorm

Beinn Liath Mhor a'Ghiubhais Li

Loch Glascarnoch

AULTGUISH

Strath Vaich

GARVE

BLACK WATER

Strath Ran noch

Little Wyvis

A. BEINN NA EUN

Ben Wyvis

Loch Glass

DINGWALL

N

Black Rock Gorge

EVANTON

5 ml
10 km

especially if it is clear and cold, there is nothing to the north you cannot see. Just across the water, the whisky hills of Aberdeen poke up provocatively with the Cairngorms behind, making Scotland seem not terribly large: the idea of walking right across it not altogether unreasonable.

The undeserving may be tempted to punish themselves with a steep and

Coire Mhor, Ben Wyvis. The suggested route runs right from the furthest corner of the loch. In early summer the easy grass still has a certain amount of easy snow lying on top Photo: Jim Teesdale

stony descent through Christmas trees followed by a plod over tarmac. David, worried about my hill speed, (unjustified: I never run with a thirty pound rucksack) had recently been doing what he called "some gentle getting fit" between Blair Atholl and Aviemore. His second day over Cairn Toul for the 5.20 train left him so exhausted that he went off by this dull way and hitched.)

The best route however is the stalkers' path north off Tom a' Choinich, which leads to a track then a path by Abhainn Beinn nan Eun (River of Ben Birds). There's a waterfall and a summer-house built by some Chinese sage for contemplation. This Chinese sage is a possessive one for it is shuttered and padlocked against informal occupancy.

Now the path tries to creep away into the heather and hide but the keen-eyed walker will manage to stay on top of it for most of the way. The route I took here - and I'll admit that it wasn't the route I'd intended to take - was up the nameless stream from GR 435753 (opposite crags) to Loch Gobhlach, then over Carn nan Con Ruadha - pleasant but tussocky. How you cross to Strath Rannoch depends on where you leave this path, which depends where *it* leaves *you*. So this section I leave as an exercise for the reader; and a good aerobic exercise it is too.

Miles are eaten on the path to Lubriach at the top of Strath Vaich. The Strath Vaich track is sadly tarmac. It would be more romantic to bash straight over the last moor and wade the river to Aultguish, but you might miss the last bar meal at 8.30.

Aultguish is overhung by its dam. There are pictures of it covered with metres of ice. When we were there it was just plain old concrete.

"Lucky you didn't come tomorrow. We've fifty fishermen booked into the bunkhouse."

"Fifty. Where are they all going to fish?"

"Well ...in the bar mostly."

Foul weather alternative: Do not miss the Black Rock Gorge but then proceed along Loch Glass to Abhainn Beinn nan Eun then the Ben Birds Path as before.

DAY 2
Aultguish to Loch a' Bhraoin
Via all the Fannichs
Distance   24 miles
Ascent   10,500 feet

And indeed, as we left the inn at 5.30, two fishermen were energetically pursuing their sport in the bar.

Higher ground is the key to the initial moor. We trudged along the road for a bit, then up through some trees onto Meallan a Gharuidhe and round the shoulder of Meall na Speireig. The little trees will eventually get bigger and I have to advise you to walk along the road a bit more (and the moor a bit less) until you can get onto the flank of the One With the Long Gaelic Name (Beinn Liath Mhor a' Ghiubhais Li). Either way the idea is to do the hard work before breakfast to leave the rest of the day clear. By breakfast David has done all he wanted to do and decided to go home. Lucky David: all the best bits of this walk are in front of him.

Sadly I hand over the Lochivraon haggis - it's too big a haggis for a lone walker. To show I'm not a mere Munro-bagger I bag the One with the Long Gaelic Name - a Corbett - and am rewarded by an aerial view of the moorlands that shows a route that is less moor than most and avoids all the peat hags.

One contour line is worth a hundred words and the one we want here is the 500 metre. Head south-westwards until you can get above it and then stay above it round to the outflow of Loch Gorm. This time I make no mistake and go right into the corrie with the lochan in it. There's a splendid old decomposing cornice above. Hmmm....splendid old decomposing cornices are best not viewed from directly below. I traverse out a bit, fill the water bottle at the wee lochan above (238689) and do all the Fannichs.

In the preamble I compared the Fannichs with the Mamores; found them to be a bit wilder, a bit rougher and with a bit less path. Still they embody the classic Scottish ridge experience, which is the closest thing you can get to flying with a thirty pound sack and heavy boots on.

If you are a sufficiently well rounded personality not to require all nine of these Munros, An Coileachan (out and back from the col) is nice enough but could be saved for another day. Beinn Liath Mhor Fannaich is a worthwhile diversion in fine weather for the view back to Sgurr Mor. A good path (not on the map) leads round from the col east of Sgurr Mor, which is jolly useful unless it's covered in hard, old snow and you don't have your ice axe. Meall a Chrasgaidh is a missable Meall but Sgurr nan Each is worth it.

As I dash back to the col for the sack:"Bagged another one then?"

How embarrassing. I am not a peak-bagger. I commune with nature and all that sort of stuff....You just got six or seven Munros rather easily but the last two make you work with a 1200ft climb out of the col. The rest of the world has retired to Aultguish, and the ridge, when you reach it, is pleasantly deserted. Descend A'Chailleach's north ridge till it flattens, then rough slopes NW to where there is a footbridge marked on the map at Lochivraon.

Not only the footbridge has gone from the top but also the river from underneath. The river has relocated a few metres to the north but the bridge is somewhere off among the Summer Isles, being a Threat to Shipping. However it's a very small river most of the time and you can always jump into the loch and swim round the end of it as Hamish Brown suggests. Contrary to rumour, the bothy itself does exist.

In the compressed coast-to-coast analogy I started off with Lochivraon corresponds to Fort William: not pretty but comfortable and very welcome. There are beds - with mattresses on! Fort William, however, does not have a dead stag lying across the entrance.

I spent the evening counting contour lines and measuring miles with my finger-joint. David had wanted to finish over the frightful pinnacles of An

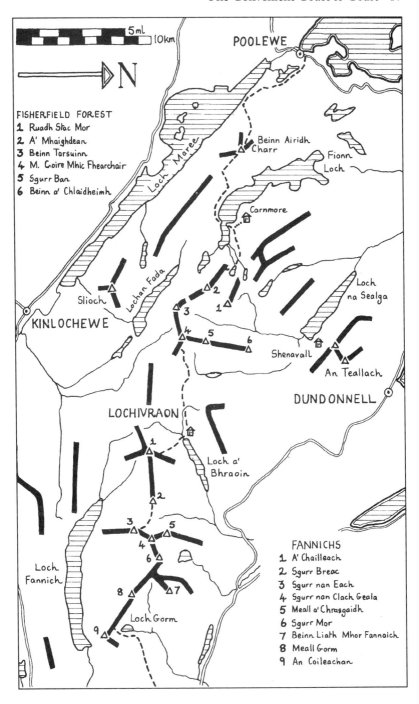

FISHERFIELD FOREST
1 Ruadh Stac Mor
2 A' Mhaighdean
3 Beinn Tarsuinn
4 M. Coire Mhic Fhearchair
5 Sgurr Ban
6 Beinn a' Chlaidheimh

FANNICHS
1 A' Chailleach
2 Sgurr Breac
3 Sgurr nan Each
4 Sgurr nan Clach Geala
5 Meall a' Chrasgaidh
6 Sgurr Mor
7 Beinn Liath Mhor Fannaich
8 Meall Gorm
9 An Coileachan

Teallach but I am a bit nervous of frightful pinnacles so I am reverting to my original idea and going straight through the middle to Poolewe.

Foul weather alternative: North side of Loch Fannich, good paths up Allt Leac a Bhealaich to col and east end of Loch a' Bhraoin.

DAY 3
Loch a' Bhraoin to Poolewe
Via Sgurr Dubh, Mullach Coire Mhic Fhearchair,
A' Mhaighdean, Carnmore Bothy, Beinn Airigh Charr
Distance   22 miles
Ascent   8900 feet

If the world was going to end on Wednesday this is how I'd spend Tuesday. On a sunny day in May it's the best walk in Scotland, which is to say in the world.

The day starts with deceptive gentleness along a riverbank, west from the loch. Do not be so captivated by the vertical things blocking off the head of the valley ahead that you miss the junction at GR 102728. The path you want doesn't fork off but starts suddenly at a small cairn on the other side of the stream.

Leave the path soon after it turns north towards Loch an Nid, once you can see into Mullach Coire Mhic Fhearchair's eastern corrie. What a corrie it is! Grim scree slopes close it off above. Lower down, rain-soaked heather has peeled off to expose bare rock. More rock walls hem you in as you climb into the corrie. Go left of these slabs (GR 073735) or over them if you want to show off the adhesion of your boot-soles.

Above the slabs a grassy gap leads up left through the crags onto the summit dome of Sgurr Dubh. Even in mist the gap will be easily found as it is the only break in the rocks apart from a couple of unattractive scree gullies. (Travelling in the opposite direction, descend with steep ground on your left until you see a tiny rock pool. You've just passed the grassy traverse line left into the corrie.)

Up through the gap, the first thing I found (well the first thing I found was an eagle: the second thing then) was a set of frightful pinnacles. By 1984 Sgurr Dubh had clambered past the three-thousand foot contour to become the second most terrifying Munro top of the mainland. As I arrived a playful snow shower was sprinkling a load of playful snow. The frightful pinnacles of Sgurr Dubh are of no difficulty but are loose and quite exposed.

On Mullach Coire Mhic Fhearchair I dropped the sack and popped over to Sgurr Ban. This shameless behaviour (I was there to commune with nature, remember) is punished with two and a half thousand feet of quartzite scree - seven hundred down, six hundred up and then back again!

Leave the Mullach on a nice sandstone ridge southwards. Usually I go over small humps on the ridge but the narrow path round the north face of Meall Garbh is a delight, dodging up and down among small outcrops. Peer round the corner from the col and you will find it. Beinn Tarsuinn, though a Munro, is on the proper line and rewards you with more frightful pinnacles. Actually these ones are pure pinnacle pleasure. The sandstone is firm and rough like your Daddy's morning chin and the places where you need your hands all have grass platforms underneath.

From the end of the ridge it's a long drop west to the col at the head of Gleann na Muice (say Mick-uh like the mouse though it means 'pigs'). In the col you cross surprisingly few peat hags. Then comes a longer climb over what, if it didn't have such a slope, would be a pleasant meadow of kingcups.

Nature in the north-west is nothing if not generous with her effects. The descent of A'Mhaighdean offers a third set of frightful pinnacles. There is an easy way off to the north, offering the extra summit of Ruadh Stac Mor.... but you've learnt your lesson now.

Apart from the pinnacles, A'Mhaighdean poses a problem of pronunciation. It is shameful to refer to such a mountain as 'the big one at the back'. Try uh-VITE-yin, meaning 'the maiden'.

The pinnacles are like clambering through the teeth of someone who hasn't been to the dentist for a long, long time. They are all too visible from the summit but in mist you will have to count paces or minutes across the plateau to find the top end. Descend into the first gap a little right (north) of the crest to get loose rock rather than loose stones. Pass below the first pinnacle to the left (south) - it overhangs all round. Climb onto the next pinnacle by either of two short chimneys on the left (south) side - an awkward move. Once you are on it there are no further difficulties.

After the pinnacles the ridge continues north west, then turn north down rocky slopes to the foot of Fuar Loch Mor (Big Cold Loch). In your post-pinnacle relaxation it is difficult not to descend the rocky slopes throwing stones at the eagles and shrieking to awaken echoes in the crags. But you restrain yourself. We who commune with nature do so in soft voices.

Go right into the corries with the Fuar Mor Lochs and Beg - I don't have to tell you that. Descend beside or inside the exit waterfall from Loch Beg but then avoid losing height as you traverse to the path; the Allt Bruthach an Easain becomes a gorge lower down.

To those of us who think that a path is a muddy trench through a bog, I explain that the stalkers' path of the Highlands is something a bit different. It has been cleverly thought out, it has been graded and it has been built. Sometimes it has primroses and violets. It is not always on the map but when it is you can recognise it by its zig-zags.

So to Carnmore Bothy, where a lonely walker with a bad knee was reading 'Touch the Void.' Lucky man not to have read that yet. He leapt up when I was still a hundred yards away to make me a cup of tea. There were rock climbers far above, visible only by their white leggings or perhaps legs - but if they'd come off they'd have arrived down the chimney of the bothy about eight seconds later. This was the last great climbing crag and, for a while, the Scottish Mountaineering Club tried to embargo the publication of any routes. This way all could experience the pioneering thrill of getting onto much harder ground than they meant to, scratching moss off the handholds, hopelessly looking for a way through that didn't exist and so on.

Wonders of the West: Slioch seen over the "frightful pinnacles" of A' Mhaighdean
Photo: Irvine Butterfield

The bold rock climbers, who came through to Carnmore in the dark, were floundering in deep peat, crying that their last hour had come. To avoid this, as well as to display a little more of the virtue of one who does not bag Munros, cross the causeway between the two lochs and climb Beinn Airigh Charr, a smallish Corbett. (Use the stalkers' path up the Strathan Buidhe until you see nice grassy slopes on the right.)

Virtue is its own reward but there are also wild goats, a top diving-board view of the sea and the best stalkers' path yet down the back. Eagle-eyed walkers will pounce on this track at the col between the Meall and the Spidean but it becomes clear and easy when you need it in the deepening heather - and there are no more frightful pinnacles - honest!

The unmetalled road above Loch Maree will take you the rest of the way but the path north of Loch Kernsary is much nicer with hardly any muddy bits. The setting sun glows green off the water and through the birch leaves to dazzle you. Loch Kernsary has a little surprise for you - it doesn't drain into the sea but backwards into Loch Maree and you must cross a final ten metre col to get out.

Poolewe appears quite suddenly: a scatter of little white houses among the rocks and bog myrtle. The finish is through some strident yellow gorse and a narrow gate onto the main street. It's so still you can smell the famous garden across the water. The sea will be lapping on the shingle beside you and the eider duck murmur softly on Loch Ewe. Enough of this; the call of the bar at Pool House is rather louder.

Foul weather alternative: a long but rewarding hike by Shenavall, Carnmore and the morass. (but beware of Abhainn Strath na Sealga in spate)

DATA FILE

Distance and Ascent

Day 0	3 miles	0 ft
Day 1	28	5100
Day 2	24	10500
Day 3	22	7600 (with Sgurr Ban 24 mls 8900 ft)
Total	77 miles	23000 ft

Time
Under Naismith's Rule the 23000 feet of ascent are equivalent to an extra 35 to 40 miles of horizontal distance. The three day crossing requires a good level of fitness, sound navigation and early starts. A crossing in 5-6 days requires a tent and a food parcel sent ahead to Aultguish (bus from Inverness 5pm Mon/Wed/Sat) That is still equivalent to 20-25 miles a day on the flat.

Terrain
Rich and varied. Stalkers' path, rough moorland, high ridges, some track but also severe rocky ground with exposed scrambling. 5 miles of tarmac at Aultguish.

Direction
Do walk east to west. The views are better, the excitement mounts instead of declining and the through-the-crags ascents of Wyvis and Sgurr Dubh would be tricky coming down.

Equipment
Walking in May, I didn't need or carry an ice-axe (other years may be different). A strong walker, I would be happy to do this one without a tent. Indeed I would make do with cold food for the single bothy night for the pleasure of moving over the ridges and pinnacles with less than twenty-five pounds up. Carry a bivvi bag; this is remote country and, if injured, you may lie twenty-four hours before rescue.

Maps
O.S. Landranger 1:50000 sheets 19, 20 and 21

Access
Access to the hills of Scotland is free to all. However this is not a right but a happy state of affairs based on the mutual respect (so far) of landowners and walkers. Camp unobtrusively and not beside the lodge at Carnmore; leave no litter and stay clear during the stalking season.

Transport
Plenty of trains to Inverness. Frequent buses via Evanton to Tain and Invergordon. From Poolewe there is an early morning bus to Inverness run by Westerbus (tel 0445 2255). This runs via Aultguish on Mondays Wednesdays and Saturdays and via Kinlochewe on Tuesdays Thursdays and Fridays. No Sunday service. From Poolewe there is also a mid morning postbus to Achnasheen, whence trains to Inverness and Skye.

Accommodation

Evanton	Novar Arms Hotel	830210
	Black Rock Camp Site	830917/867
	B & B's and shops	
Aultguish	Aultguish Inn (& Bunkhouse)	255
Nest of Fannich	Bothy burnt down.	
Loch a' Bhraoin	Lochivraon Bothy.	
Shenavall	Bothy, crowded at weekends (6 mls north of route but on foul weather alternative.)	
Carnmore	Bothy, crowded at weekends.	
Poolewe	Pool House Hotel	272
	Poolewe Hotel	241
	National Trust for Scotland Camp Site	249
	B & B's & shops	

I used the Back Rock Campsite, Aultguish Bunkhouse, Lochivraon Bothy and NTS Campsite. I had bar meals at the Novar Arms, Aultguish Inn and the Pool House. All were good - the Pool House was excellent.

Reference

Tourist Info.	Ross and Cromarty. Tel. 01463 73505 for useful accommodationbooklet, bus knowledge etc.
Yellow Pages	'Highland' under Guest Houses and B & B's
Weather	Met Office Northern Highlands 2 Day 01891500425

Chapter Two
THE TWO TOPS
Stonehaven to Portree

Almost anybody can find a good high-level line in Scotland. Look up the Munros and Corbetts, open out the map to find the ridges and then walk along them. A good low-level line needs more planning, more local knowledge and not a little luck. On this route we were lucky. Our green bits turned out to be woods not plantations and many of our paths turned out to exist. Our mix of valley, upland and mountain, tough ground and fast, balanced well in the end.

The Two Tops is a long crossing - 280 miles and 45000 feet of climb, though you could end it at Glenelg and still have a solid coast to coast. Apart from the Two of the title, 16 Munros are crossed as well as an accidental Corbett. It could be done without a tent but you would have to book a room at least one day in advance and undertake some fairly tough days: Tomdoun to Suardalan Bothy over nine Munros being the real decider.

I shall imbed enough route description amongst the anecdotes and chitchat to allow you to follow the line in detail. You will still need reasonable fitness, sound equipment and enough general map skill to understand contour lines and find north-west in mist.

David and I walked it in the summer after our Southern Upland Way. I planned as far as Fort Augustus, David the rest. The week before we left we discovered that our bold concept was not entirely original. An article in The Times revealed that Chris Brasher and two hundred and forty-nine others

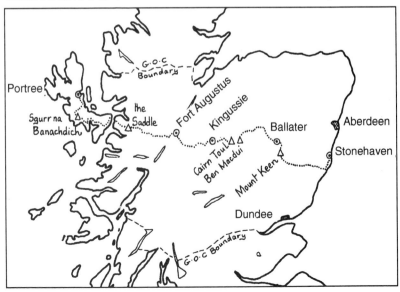

were at that very moment walking coast to coast on something they called the Ultimate Challenge.

DAY 0
Stonehaven

There is an alarming downpour outside the windows of the train but, bent over our maps, we are able to ignore the real world. My half of the route includes Mount Keen, which is the most easterly Munro, and so David has responded with Sgurr na Banachdich on Skye, which is the most westerly one. (And yes this original concept too has been anticipated by Hamish Brown...)

Despite our rather different ideas of what should go into a rucksack both of them weighed 24lb, excluding food. Over the subsequent five years, with all the advances in lightweight gear, this weight has mysteriously stayed exactly the same. David has brought the tent; so much for my efforts to devise a route with accommodation. We uncover a schedule error. We are to cross to Skye by the Glenelg ferry on Day Eleven, Sunday 11th June. The Glenelg ferry doesn't run on Sundays.

Evening sunlight bounces off squares of yellow rape seed. From the train we cannot see any hills at all. Cullen Skink is off at the Marine Hotel so we have a marine meal of crab and shark instead. David is on a hypnotherapeutic diet; it is not clear how he will find in the Highlands 4500 calories of raw food daily. Tomorrow he plans early sea-bathing; now he looks out of the window over the harbour and wonders if he should be taking a sailing holiday instead. I offer to take photos of the sea-bathing for I carry too little subcutaneous fat for cold swims.

DAY 1
Stonehaven to Auchenblae
Howe o' the Mearns
15 ½ miles 700 feet; 8 hours

Howe o' Mearns is the farming country behind Stonehaven immortalized in Lewis Grassic Gibbons 'Sunset Song', which I have in my sack. David has Boswell and Dr Johnson travelling in the Highlands.

A path leaves the southern corner of the harbour and rises to a clifftop for an interesting scramble to Downie Point. The amusing path continues up and down and even through the cliff to Dunnottar Castle. This is the brooding essence of all a castle should be with a history of sieges, massacres and thrilling escapes. It also has one of the world's truly thrilling loos (unfortunately gents only) perched on the extreme corner of the clifftop with nesting kittiwakes ten feet away through the window. Among the conveniences of which I have availed myself, only the one at the Cabane des Vignettes in the Valais Alps, with its two-thousand foot drop onto the glacier, is more vertiginous.

The next bit south along the clifftop is a scenic diversion to avoid miles of forest road. It is heavy going. David in his "braw legs" shorts has trouble with

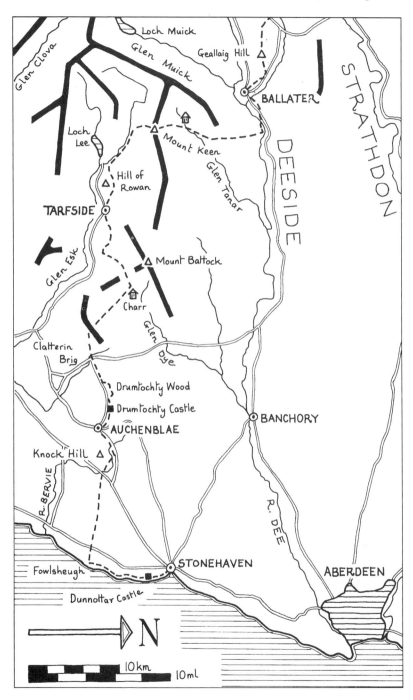

nettles, which flourish along the fertile strip between fields of barley and oilseed rape and giddy 150 foot drops into the sea. When we stop for lunch we have covered just 3 miles in 4 hours. We now pass 1 1/2 miles x 200 feet of guillemot dung. The cliff face, originally brown, carries a layer of white guano, covered with a layer of grey guillemots. The guano odour makes our Scottish Cheddar taste like very ripe dolcalette.

From Crawton we make our way inland on minor roads by Mill of Barras and Nether Pitforthie with just a short section of path leading to Gyratesmyre Farm. This section while hard on the legs is very easy on the nose; the air is sharp with salt and sweet with early gorse.

An unusual two-lane tarmac footbridge takes us over the Bervie; we could visit the Court Stone (776796) but it's just a stone in the middle of a field of soaking wet barley so we don't. An interesting footbridge on the map tempts us over the hill to Glenbervie but the bridge isn't that interesting and another time I would traverse the ridge of Knock Hill to avoid the road bit into Auchenblae. The final entry into the village is by the track through Myreside Farm, some slight relief from the road. Fifteen miles shouldn't be tiring; maybe I measured it too short. We have one large blister each - oh dear.

Auchenblae has a steeply-sloping main street, a few shops and two hotels. The hotels are both fairly seedy. David laughs at my lightweight evening outfit. I explain, untruthfully, that the reason my trouser-bottoms don't reach my feet is that I cut them off to save weight. He buys us some pork scratchings - for me, with my sheltered rural lifestyle, a new gourmet experience. We follow them with golden turkey nuggets, another novel taste sensation. There were four of the nuggets, each filled with exploding pink cheese.

We make a dusk visit to the cemetery chapel with sixteenth-century gravestones and a sinister crypt. It is good practice for the shelter stone.

Dunnottar Castle, sinister start-point for the walk.

DAY 2
Auchenblae to Tarfside
Into the Highlands
22 miles 2500 feet 9 1/2 hours

For the first half-mile there's a lovely riverside path on the east bank of the Luther. It's peculiarly satisfying to find a foot-passage into the heart of a built-up area. A farm track (we could have done with some of this yesterday) leads round to Drumtochty Castle. The private signs around the castle had all fallen down so we went through, reassuring each other that a private road may be a public footpath. The castle hides among shrubbery, showing only a flagpole; maybe it's ashamed of being a nineteenth-century imitation.

We climbed a totally unnecessary forest trail north of the road to find a pool all hung with elder trees. From the top of the pool the trail traverses westward to a viewpoint, from which a neglected and unmarked track leads forward and down through vivid green beech trees.

Two final miles of road led to Clatterin' Brig, which is a twentieth-century imitation. Here we crossed the Highland Line and, though grassy banks of the Back Burn took us a little way in, almost at once we were climbing steeply through heather and within the hour had spotted fifty red deer. Once over the shoulder of Hound Hillock on what the map supposes is a path, the flat lands were forgotten; we could be anywhere east of Drumochter. This land is pisted and groomed for killing grouse. Tiny grouse chicks scattered in front of us, beeping anxiously like reversing trucks.

We took lunch in the beautifully constructed shooters' hut at the bottom of the Hangy Burn. Long, fast Landrover tracks lead onward past the abandoned house at Charr. This would be a handy bothy, I thought as we went by. Later I wrote to the Mountain Bothies people and said so. The owner said yes; some prisoners from Perth Gaol came in and spruced it up and now this simple unlocked shelter is waiting for you to come and sleep in it.

Unless you want to turn right up the Burn of Badymicks (GR 588833) and bag Mount Battock, the easternmost Corbett, take the track up the Water of Dye for another non-existent path over the Hill of Turret.

Only a few drops of rain had fallen on us but tendrils of damp were rising off the ridges like spindrift snow. This weird effect we were to view from inside in the Cairngorms. We met a couple, Bob and Mary, on their way from Mrs. Guthrie's. They warned of snow in the Lairig Ghru!

The next track leads down by the Burn of Turret to the road but we turn right just in time for the path   past Blackcraigs and north of Craig Crane. David is tired, the peewits and lapwings very noisy. They seem to be getting on his nerves. We descend onto Tarfside via Cairncross ... and Mrs Guthrie at the Parsonage.

This place carried no advertisements, had no phone, not even a board outside the house, but, reasoning that there had to be somewhere to stay in Glen Esk, I rang for help the only number in the tourist booklet - the folk museum. Mrs. Guthrie turned out to be one of the great hillwalking B & B's. During the previous week's Ultimate Challenge, sixty-one had tea and covered the lawn around the church with tents. We find a signed copy of Hamish Brown's 'The Great Walking Adventure' and read all about his Ultimate Challenge.

"When would you like your supper boys?"

"About seven o' clock"

"Oh no; you'll need longer than that to finish your tea."

A huge home-baked tea is immediately followed by a mince and tatties supper. "Scots have the highest rate of heart disease in the world," says David, disparaging this ethnic largesse.

"Yes, but only because the hillwalking diet is out of step with the office-sitting lifestyle." Sadly, ill-health means that Mrs Guthrie no longer offers hillwalkers just what they need most - lots of food; alternative arrangements are in place during Challenge week only.

DAY 3
Tarfside to Ballater
Over Mount Keen
21 miles 2600 feet; 8 hours

Powered by Mrs. Guthrie's high octane breakfast, off we go up the westward path with a cloud of black smoke coming out the back. Rabbits in hundreds live in these low fields. David takes the path round the north side of Rowan Hill but I go over the top, where there's a thirty-foot conical monument to nothing in particular. It has a triangular doorway with an uncomfortable little room inside.

Esk is a splendid glen and the meeting point of hill paths in five directions, although for people in cars it's a long dead end. Invermark, today's castle, has its doorway ten feet up so we do some rock-climbing to get in. Down inside there's a barrel vaulted cellar with shafts of light through the ground-level slits, which the defenders would have used to shoot you in the kneecaps as you stood around outside.

We take the Mounth Road north-westwards up onto Mount Keen. This is a popular highway, with the army, schemers under the Duke of Edinburgh and a scattering of ordinary human beings. The track is high and stony, built for feet not wheels, even if the feet were originally those of black cattle.

Don Whillans, Joe Brown and Dougal Haston meet on the summit in the shape of rucksacks - mine, David's and the bloke who took our summit photo. Don Whillans is the youngest of the three at fifteen years. Did these famous climbers ever meet in real life? Perhaps on the Old Man of Hoy - I cannot imagine they would have bothered with Mount Keen, though it does have good views: behind, the distant sea and ahead, Lochnagar and the Cairngorms.

On Mount Keen I pick up a stone, which I intend to leave on Sgurr na Banachdich. This involves rock-climbing and David has sent a rope ahead to Skye. Mount Keen is my first Munro for eleven years.

Just a few drops of rain fall on us as we continue north, taking the track along Glen Tanar to Etnach (GR 416915). Our first ptarmigan squawk out,

Mount Keen, the first of the Two Tops and a typical less interesting Eastern Munro.

and two mountain bikes, moving much slower than the ptarmigan and not seeming to have much fun. This is the quiet side of the hill, with just the sound of boots in heather and long grey slopes leading down to the Dee. We switch around from hill to track to path to reach the bend of the Dee near Headinch.

The woods ahead are green and trembling with wide stretches of river and an exciting moment. The Dee is so wide that the O. S. footbridge symbol only gets half way across. Will the footbridge do the same? White ironwork shows through the birches. It does exist and is the finest river-crossing yet restored, repainted and re-opened by the Queen Mother a few months before. (No of course she didn't do the painting!)

We call it an abandoned railway but they call it a scenic walkway. Either way it takes you rejoicing into Ballater with its broom and its larch and its edifying notices explaining Byron, geology and dark Lochnagar.

I had brought us round here to study the Souterrain, our fourth underground chamber and another one in anticipation of the Shelter Stone, but we have sore feet. Because we have sore feet we have to hurry; we are out of moleskin. Tomorrow is Sunday and after the that we shall see no shops until Kingussie.

We reach Ballater at 4.50 PM. A chemist, due to close at 5.00, has but a single slice of moleskin and some extra thick bunion protector.

"Go to the other chemist and, if they don't have it, get them to ring me and I will stay open for you to come back for the bunion stuff."

Happily the other place has both. Meanwhile David has been exploring the town for food and, under some sudden inspiration buys a haggis. After drinking milk alfresco style in the town park we make our way to the Youth Hostel, a seedy place with a front lawn that needs mowing. We have a slap up

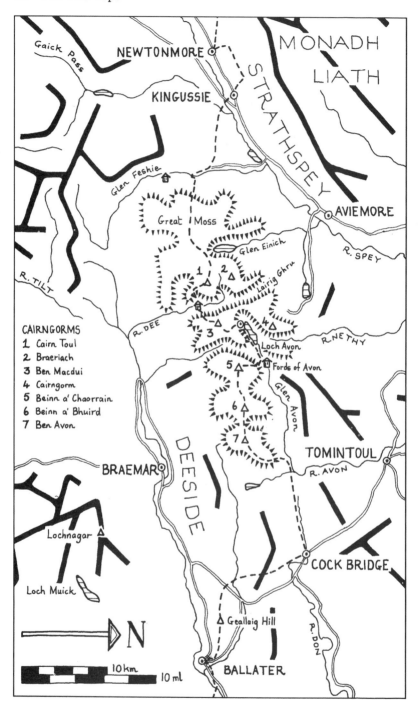

bar meal of snails and venison. It's Saturday night in Ballater; the fat young women are gorgeously dressed and the fat young men wear dirty old jeans. Between the two is a narrow alley full of legs leading to the loo. One of the fat girls has a fag up her nose - it's all a bit urban for us.

At the Youth Hostel they say there's hardly any snow on Beinn a' Bhuird.

DAY 4
Ballater to Cock Bridge
Dee to Don
14 miles, 3000 feet

David quotes from Boswell's travels. Boswell told Voltaire he was off to Scotland and Voltaire looked at him as if he had said the North Pole. Of course this has lost much of its point now that the North Pole is so accessible.

The Youth Hostel in the clear morning light is even seedier; breath condenses in the cold dormitory and the head falls off David's broom. I make a full loaf of marmalade sandwiches; it seems the convenient way to carry the marmalade.

We go out to the River Dee through the grounds of an hotel and across the golf course, thwacked guttapercha whizzing about our ears. A better way to the river, however, is from the bridge on the B976. This is a railway, not derelict but simply never built; Queen Victoria didn't want the trains passing the bottom of her garden. Here is a romantic suicide spot, 'The Postie's Leap'; I hurry David past on his bad feet, lest he is tempted to follow the postie over.

Impulsively, to save those feet from the hard road, I decide on the enterprising high route over Geallaig Hill. A grassy track past Culsh Farm (GR 345978) passes birch and juniper. I also spot two fawns bouncing about in a field. David stops to botch his feet with the bunion protector. Geallaig turns out to be well tracked, alive with hares and covered with remnants of the Caledonian Forest. At 2440 feet it's just too small for a Corbett; so much the better for it. On the summit, a potential tragedy: my rucksack strap breaks off. Poor old Joe Brown. I'll fix it for now with a spare strap. Will it last the three days to Kingussie? Fortunately, as a true rural type, I have plenty of binder-twine.

We head north west to cross the old military road at Braenaloin and take the track northward, turning right to cross the Gairn at Tullochmacarrick; this track becomes a heather bash over a pass, unused for twenty years, east of Camock Hill. It may be that the alternative path by Easter Sleach exists.

Thirty deer arrange themselves along the skyline in the way that deer are supposed not to do. Here, as on the shoulder of Mount Battock on Day 2, the hags are so dry that we can walk along alleys of brown peat with our heads at the level of the heather. At the top the lochan has dried up too; it is a pavement of pale peat with polygonal cracks like the ones you get in the Tundra. I try walking out on it but it wobbles so I go back. Two kestrels soar, yelping. If the deer were surprised to see us, these birds are definitely cross. With some relief we reach a track where I find two extra lengths of binder twine. David doesn't understand that the true rural type cannot have too much binder-twine. We realize when we find half-bridges of mortarless stone that the track is a grown-over road of General Wade. We shall cross more of these bridges on Speyside; they are well enough built that even half of one is strong enough to cross.

We track north-west towards Cock Bridge and, where my map shows a Youth Hostel, find Jenny's Hut. At £3.50 it's rather attractive and her tepee tent even more so, at a fee she hasn't decided as she's only just finished putting it up. But David has his mind fixed on bathtime at the Allargue Arms.

Cock Bridge is a minute clump of habitation among the hills and a seven-teenth-century castle in the 1960's brutalist style. It has been a tiring day: we remeasure but it will not come to more than fourteen miles.

At the Allargue Arms we find that the Ultimate Challenge has been before us; Chris Brasher is in the visitors' book. David, still reading Boswell, says that I must record his *bons mots* in this diary. I say that I have been waiting for some. He says my face is tanned and that I look positively attractive. I find this outrageously witty and intelligent and transcribe it quickly before I forget it. Actually my face is pink, especially the cheek that's been facing south.

Foul weather alternative: From Ballater a track, then a path, then a minor road lead up the east side of the Gairn to Lary. Take the path through Glen Fenzie, then two and a half miles of the A939. Now you can follow the previously mentioned military road.

DAY 5
Cock Bridge to the Shelter Stone
Into the Cairngorms
23 miles 5500 feet 10 hours

We leave at nine along a tiny metalled estate road south of the River Don. It takes us into big hills from which we will not emerge for two days. Our intended one up Glen Avon is longer than yesterday's route, which we found quite long enough. I am therefore impressed when David proposes diverting over the two large hills to the south. We descend into the green hollow of the hills at Inchrory and do that.

A track leads up the end of Ben Avon, approximately where the path is on the map. It makes a final flick and drops us off onto the best Cairngorm ter-rain - dwarf heather and low arctic mosses to walk on, craggy slopes fading in and out of the mist and neat granite outcrops poking out of the plateau. Between brisk showers the Big Brae steams like freshly dropped dung of the ancestral cow. (Actually it is horse-manure that steams in this way but the idea of the Cairngorms being dropped out by a horse seems not quite right. An Ancestral Elephant maybe?)

The summit is perfect, a granite tor. A distant town is identified with the compass as Braemar. Beinn a' Bhuird, after a good col leading to it, is less interesting - a shapeless lump. Fortunately the top's at this end. A little snow falls on us - but it's the fifth of June! Yes, but the Cairngorms it is. For some

The grand lines of Ben Avon are contradicted by its frivolous summit rocks

reason David feels we should now climb Beinn a' Chaorrain as well: perhaps he has Munro fever. Beinn a Chaorrain is a nasty hill. The name means Hill of the Rowan Tree but there isn't a tree within ten miles of the thing. It is defended not by crags but by steep boulder-fields and wide, flat bogs.

On our way down the north ridge, sleet begins to fall in earnest; it becomes wet snow as we trudge up the south side of Loch Avon under various spectacular precipices. We wonder what happens if we cannot find the Shelter Stone. Fortunately the Shelter Stone is easy to find. It's big, it looks like its picture and the path goes right in through the door.

It's seven in the evening and we are good and wet. David has worn shorts through the sleet. He is very cold, but has a precious pair of dry trousers in the sack. So he thinks; but both rucksacks have let in water, particularly Joe Brown, who is not big enough for this job.

Haggis and instant mash is, we discover, what the gods eat up in the sky; even a Cup-a-Soup prompts tributes too extravagant for any advertisement. At the time I was unable to believe that so deeply rewarding an experience could be purchased for nine pence.

As I crouch over the stream to wash up (the instant mash has already sucked up most of the haggis grease) I am awed by huge cloudy crags all around. Loch Avon (pronounced Arn) is a very high one at 2400 feet but it is surrounded by four-thousand foot mountains. Even going back out by the river from its foot, it's nineteen miles to the first inhabited house. We have put our heads into a bag nineteen miles deep. Tomorrow we will have to break out through those four-thousanders.

I have always wanted to sleep at the Shelter Stone but sometimes the gods give us more than we wanted; in this case, the Shelter Stone with snow on top. Disadvantages: it's dark, it's cold and the roof is very low. Advantages: it's dry and it's roomy. We sleep very well considering.

Foul weather alternative: In thick weather the cliffs of Garbh Coire are waiting to swallow the incompetent compass-user. Take the track and path up Glen Avon by way of the bothy at Faindouran. After heavy rain the Fords of Avon may be impassable; If this is the case go up the north side of Loch Avon and circle the head of the Loch.

DAY 6
Shelter Stone to Kingussie
Out of the Cairngorms
26 miles 5500 feet 12½ hours

During the night a mouse has broken into our porridge. The life of a Shelter Stone mouse doesn't bear thinking about. It's still sleeting and we have a bit of a lie-in, hoping for it to stop. It doesn't so it's back into our wet clothes and off at nine-thirty.

A rocky path leads round the base of the Shelter Stone Crag and up to Loch Etchachan. It sounds big and impressive, although we can only see a few feet of grey waves as we circle its shores and take a careful bearing up onto Ben Macdui. And on Ben Macdui, a blizzard!

Now come two really nasty hours. There's nine inches of fresh snow on the boulders. The map starts falling to pieces and my hands go numb; I have gloves but they are not heavy-duty mountaineering ones.

We reach the cairn at twelve-thirty, having covered three miles of the day's twenty-six in three and a half hours. It would be sensible to flee north to Aviemore. In Aviemore I could even buy a new rucksack. A thousand feet down - we're on the slope just south of the Allt Clach nan Taillear - the wind

A fine day on the Macdui plateau. To reach Cairn Toul (behind) we must drop 2000 feet into Lairig Ghru. From Cair Toul it's another 15 miles to suppertime. East to west is the hard way to cross the Cairngorms.   *Photo: Jim Teesdale*

drops, the sun peers out and it is not snowing or even raining so we'll go for Cairn Toul as planned. Down, down into the deep trough of Lairig Ghru. They ski this, they think it's fun. Even David thinks it might be quite fun.

We have crossed some interesting footbridges this trip - stone arches on Donside, the Queen Mother's at Cambus o' May- and here is a new sort of one across the Upper Dee. The footway is a high arch, tied together across the base with two steel rods. It's a bowstring girder, just like the Sydney Harbour Bridge only smaller and built by the engineering department at Aberdeen. It looks absurdly light but has stood since 1951.

With a long-distance pack, it is a good solid pull of 2500 feet to Cairn Toul from the Corrour Bothy but on top the sun is shining and the wind has completely gone. The contrast with Ben Macdui two miles and three and a half hours away across the deep divide of Lairig Ghru is hard to believe. Now it is all downhill to Kingussie, which is just as well for it's already four o' clock.

On the high wild waste of the Great Moss you could put up a tent anywhere over twenty square miles; next year David will plan his Ultimate Challenge route to do just that. Cairn Toul is two mountains. From the other side it is a great jagged peak overlooking the Lairig, but from here it is just a high point at the edge of this rolling grassland, which once went on forever before the glaciers started gnawing at its edges.

Two walkers with a tent come up out of the craggy hole of Glen Einich - the first people we've seen for two days. We pass Loch nan Cnapan and find the end of the track, soon leaving it for the path towards Carn Ban Mor. We hope Carn Ban Mor's not a Munro because we cannot be bothered to climb the extra thirty metres...(It used to be but not anymore. Hamish Brown crossed it off in 1984.)

The path is a very old one. Its little cairns every forty yards are quite useless as the moss has grown up around them until only the top stone of each is still showing. It dives off the edge of the plateau, passes below an 'S' shaped patch of snow and drops into Glen Feshie. Having by chance taken the lower path, we arrive at Achleum through steep pinewood with a waterfall running down through it - charming wood number six.

It's still seven miles more into Kingussie. The first half-mile is up (not down) - Glen Feshie for the footbridge, then by forest roads with only the bit of open grazing land between Corarnstilmore (GR 832983) and Baileguish to relieve the blue-green monotony. It might be bearable if you could amble and stop, change into dry socks and eat an orange perhaps, but we had to press down hard on our sore feet if we were to get food and a roof over our heads at Kingussie.

Coming down through the trees we crossed the 1000 foot contour for the first time since the birch and juniper wood outside Ballater. We hit the Youth Hostel at ten.

"Sorry we're so late. Delayed by a blizzard on Ben Macdui."

"Yes: your money's damp."

Apparently it has been snowing in Kent. Here, the long evening trudge into the westering sun has burnt the fronts of my ears, which seems unfair.

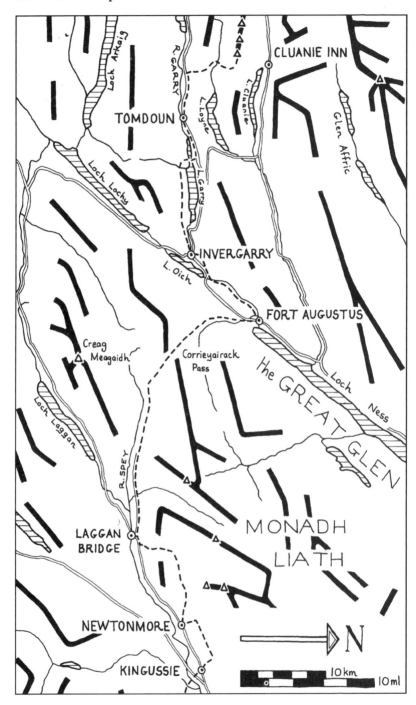

We eat from tins, wash our socks, wash our feet and are in bed with the lights out by eleven as SYHA rules require.

The next three days are easy ones but then there's a plunge into the Cluanie Hills.

Foul weather alternative: half the fun of the Shelter Stone is that there isn't any way out except over the top. If you have supplies for an extra day you can go downstream from Loch Etchachan to Derry Lodge and then by White Bridge to upper Glen Feshie.

Only a strong party will reach Ruigh Aiteachain bothy in a day. If supplies are low, the only escape is by the north side of Loch Avon, The Saddle and Strath Nethy to Loch Morlich. Paths through the ancient pines of Rothiemurchs lead by Loch an Eilein and Feshiebridge to Kingussie.

DAY 7
Kingussie to Laggan Bridge
Speyside
15 miles; 600 feet; 8 hours

Kingussie Youth Hostel, unlike Ballater, boasts various palatial features: elegant colonnades, pre-Raphaelite stained glass, a tiled veranda, and a drying room (well surely palaces have drying rooms)? We start slowly, off at ten after a fine, all-grease breakfast provided by David. We continue the same way, northwards beside the river and over a footbridge onto the edge of the golf course.

We already know mountains but these bits of lowland are a treat; here's yet another woodland path beside Loch Gynack. We walk along the south shore of this loch, then right a bit to the edge of a plantation; open ground leads to a man-high cairn at GR 713000, which marks the top of the path down to Newtonmore.

They don't sell rucksacks in Newtonmore. We omit the Clan Macpherson Museum in favour of a pub. The gentlemen in the bar pass sexual innuendoes on David's legs - he's very pleased.

"Actually they do look rather good don't they?"

It is hard to get out of the pub: not just unwilling legs but a large, black, woolly dog sprawled across the doorway.

A bit of road and then another wild, lonely Landrover track leads up Glen Banchor - perhaps one lonely Landrover track too many. Maybe we should be climbing Munros to the north: bleak and unknown hills with dull names; Gaelic has twenty-seven ways of saying the Rounded Brownish Mound.

At the head of the Strathe an Eilich is another unusual footbridge (GR 648985): its central pier consists of three oildrums filled with concrete. Here also is an unattractive bothy with sofa and empty whisky bottles. We cross the bridge and head down the Strath. Cluny Castle at the bottom of the track is another pile surrounded by rhododendrons and 'Private' signs. I would not bother with it but leave the track to head south westwards across-bog for Laggan. The Monadliath Hotel has a ruined church in the garden - most odd. Only two more days before David's mighty Cluanie one; this has been a short one but tomorrow is a good twenty-six miler.

DAY 8
Laggan Bridge to Fort Augustus
Corrieyairack Pass
26 miles; 1400 feet

The weather is still excellent, cool with occasional showers. David manages five steps from the hotel before the first footcare stop. All but two of his nine blisters are better now but his ankle has swollen to the size of a knee. So much for handsome legs.

Going shopping at Laggan means we miss the footpath along the south bank of the Spey but I divert to the iron-age fort, Dun-da-Lamh (GR 583930). There is a good path slanting up off the forest road; a steep climb through larch and scots pine. Why is it that scots pine plantations are less offensive than spruce? Is it that they make us think of the real Caledonian Forest of the Cairngorms? So if I'd taken a few walks in Alaska I'd find I rather liked the acres of Sitka Spruce.

The fort is impressive; you can see the collapsed remains of quite a lot of Pictish stonework. Also much countryside: it's a small hill in the middle of a valley, like Rowan Hill in Glen Esk and Geallaig on Deeside. I take a last photo of the S-shaped patch of snow in Glen Feshie; we've been trying to walk away from it since Tuesday.

I go down the grassy side of the Dun and back to the road. Now I must catch up with David; this shouldn't be too hard; he's extremely slow today. Below Sherrabeg I escape the road for the lochside and cross a footbridge of a single sandstone slab. The road needs escaping - there's a lot of it.

At the head of the reservoir there's a Wade bridge with not only no road over it anymore but no river under either. I cross over then under it to create a weird topographical loop in the Two Tops Walk and also to look at the stonework. The masons used undressed stone straight off the hill - quicker but much more skilful.

"No buses up there mate!" quips a stroller with an English city accent.

He's wrong. A red Landrover postbus overtakes me. Returning, it offers to take me back up its route to David.

"No, he cannot be far ahead now."

The tarmac continues. Beside it, David has left little cairns decorated with beer cans and bindertwine, a reference to the useful lengths I have in my rucksack, which he somehow finds amusing.

Across Garva Bridge and it's still tarmac. Nine miles of it and it's too much. At its end David has stopped for me at an informal bothy - the lunch is in my sack. Instead of a visitors' book the bothy has scribbling on the walls. Some go back to 1977.

General Wade didn't build drains but his bridges are lovely. Clearly he was a man for the Imaginative Route Choice; was it really necessary to climb to 2500ft to get through hills rising to only 2940? Road and then pylons up the pass mean that you have to use a bit of imagination to get the full flavour of this perverse crossing - unless the mist's down of course! All four feet are battered and blistered although David's right is less bad than the rest. Pain and pylons can't spoil the final zig-zag mile up the headwall of a corrie that's like the Back of Nowhere itself. As you top the pass a wonderful view leaps from the other side and hits you between the eyes. From North to South, sixty miles of new western hills stretch themselves out before us; behind them the sea - and Skye. We meet two parties moving east over the pass. They have come from the coast in three days and tell of a wonder bunkhouse at COUGIE in Glen Affric. It's got free showers - free HOT showers! They stayed last night with the monks in Fort Augustus.

The long descent from the pass is very lovely in the afternoon sun but it really does for our feet. Three people are lying in the grass above the track waiting for the right light to photograph the new model Range Rover. They have a garden sprayer to make it glisten. In the evening, Loch Ness stretches away forever. At GR 384044 we take a path right, which is actually a grass track through the nicest wood so far (nice wood number 12), with tall, tall birches and a tumbling stream. Our feet are too sore to enjoy it. The path emerges near Culachy House and so do we at seven.

David insists on claiming the hospitality of the Abbey; he once imposed himself on the Bishop of Limpopo and had to speak French at dinner. The schoolboys are playing tennis. One of them goes for a monk - it is most embarrassing. A monk arrives but they are full up. We find B&B with Mrs McLean at Victoria Cottage. Our meal at the Gallery Restaurant is so awful it cheers us up. The food is cold, the carrots have brown bits on, the service is slow and the place is empty (no wonder). These people have gone to real trouble with their badness; the table is decorated with three dead flowers and the taped music of Stevie Wonder emerges from a battery-powered cassette recorder.

We shall take a rest day at Fort Augustus and I'll go to Fort William for a rucksack. If the feet are no better by Tomdoun I'm going home, for this is no fun at all and it's not even raining.

DAY 9
Fort Augustus/Fort William
rest day

We have a wonderful vanitory unit: oval and kidney-shaped: white with gold twiddles, three oval mirrors, and legs like David's. Mrs McLean speaks sadly of depopulation. There were summer pastures up in Corrieyairack. Thousands lived in these valleys but they all went to Canada. She speaks as if all this were yesterday. It was one hundred and fifty years ago.

We inspect sailing craft; watching the boats go through the locks is the main summer pastime in Fort Augustus. I go to Fort William and buy a big blue rucksack for £64.50. In Fort William I learn interesting facts about General Wade's roads. The soldiers who built them got sixpence extra a day. They dug fifteen feet wide down to firm ground, however deep, and (because they didn't have surveyors?) in straight lines. The straight lines are very obvious in Corrieyairack. This however means that there are many hollows where the snows drift and that was the main defect of the roads. Captain Edward Burt wrote at the time:

> "The objections made by some among the Highlanders are that the bridges in particular will render the ordinary people effeminate."

Also the gravel was too hard for unshod Highland Ponies. For us too!

In Fort William is a lock of Bonnie Prince Charlie's golden hair and a picture of him as Flora MacDonald's maid with a pistol in his knickers. "If anybody looks as close as me as that," he said, "I shall get found out anyway". He made a pretty maid, but that was just the artist. In fact he was midge-bitten, covered with scorbutic sores and drunk.

"I haven't ironed them", Mrs. McLean apologizes as she gives back the clothes she's put through the washing machine for us.

DAY 10
Fort Augustus to Tomdoun
Glengarry
19 miles 800 feet

From here on the route has been planned by David. We go out past the locks on the towpath along the north side of the Caledonian Canal. He gazes longingly at a hundred and twenty ton yacht thing, "Lucrezia Johanna". Again he's wondering if he shouldn't have been on a boating holiday - our legs are still sadly defective. We go for four miles between canal and river. The feet may be poor but the ground below them is good, dripping with gorse and hawthorn. It even smells good and, with water on both sides, is enjoyably unlike mountains. We race the "Lucrezia", catching up whenever she stops at a lock, and they film us with their video cameras from the deck..... at this very moment innocent strangers in Denmark may be wondering at our strange pastimes and admiring our legs.

Loch Oich smells of dead fish. One and a half miles of main road beside Loch Oich cannot be avoided: then a forest road slants up right, with a descent track left after the power lines to Invergarry. Cross straight over the A87 on a track that bridges the Garry and take a path up the river's south bank. A really special footbridge goes back across the Garry, a perfect replica of the Sydney Harbour Bridge: sadly it is not necessary to cross it. The riverside footpath crosses the A82. Where it reaches the minor road (281005) near a Forestry Enterprise car park, take the forest road to the west.

Here we divert along the nature Trail Trail, which turns out badly; we lose the marked path and have to shove our way through low spruce trees (we should have followed the map, not the markers; the path is there, marked 'Nature Trail'.) Penetrating small spruce with a big sack is more energetic than man-hauling sledges across the arctic. David is definitely annoyed (the diversion is my fault) and refuses to eat lunch by a really first class waterfall. We are not allowed to have lunch whilst we are still lost.

The trail reappears. As a concession to educational value, there is a sign, "Birch", under one of the birch trees. We pass Loch Garry on grassy tracks without seeing it at all. Our first midges join us over our delayed lunch. And it still isn't raining.

The track passes Greenfield and we take a right fork to make a fine crossing of the narrow bit of Loch Garry on a bridge, which is a meccano box girder with a concrete floor. Still, it's the first one over a loch. Two and a half miles of tarmac road lead to Tomdoun Hotel, which is pronounced Tomdown.

There is a bunkhouse but we're booked into the proper place. It is a wonderful Victorian hunting lodge with battered hardwood furniture, brass taps, soppy Victorian engravings and a photo of King Edward in his kilt. And under the brass taps - at last, a proper bath; the first since Mrs. Guthrie's. A curse on the person who invented the shower.

David has some battered and deep-fried nameless lumps, dredged from the bottom of the North Sea. "Better left there," he says. His feet must still be bad. The bar is decorated with fish that people have killed and the staircase has a display of bullets. The place is full of Munro-baggers, including one who has bagged his last and is drinking champagne. A horse race arrives from the pony place down the glen. It's wet as it has just forded the wide River Garry.

The weather forecast for tomorrow is poor to foul. We have 7000 feet of ascent along the Cluanie Ridge. It will be the feet at the bottom of the legs, though, that give us trouble. The hotel has a wonderful map consisting of nine O.S. sheets. We trace exploits current and to come. The new Munroist says "what you're doing sounds a lot better than the Ultimate Challenge. Sgurr na Banachdich is not too hard though considerably different to Mount Keen."

David has got a foul-smelling cigarillo from somewhere - I don't think I was meant to see it. The reason for his 60% raw food and Evian water diet is to give up smoking as he's accidentally restarted. He's has managed virtually no raw food on this trip although there was a limp salad with the nameless lumps.

DAY 11
Tomdoun to Sgurr na Sgine
The South Cluanie Ridge
18 miles 7500 feet 10 3/4 hours

The waitresses have all been out for their Saturday night (where to, we wondered?) so there is no chance of an early breakfast for us. However, porridge and Loch Fyne kipper are worth waiting for and we get away at 9.15. It's another cloudy-bright day.

A beige spaniel comes with us along the road. That'll soon go home we think but it follows us for seven miles, keeping skilfully just out of range of the stones I have in my pocket to throw at it. I imagine leading the dog on a piece of my useful bindertwine into Glenelg Police Station with a note for the hotel saying "I don't know if your dog is a Munro-bagger but she's just done the Cluanies." We and the dog go for three miles along the road, then up the path beside the Allt a Ghobhainn. The path's a delight, the pebbles striped and speckled with no two the same - schist probably. North we go through the pass and down into Glen Loyne, where she leaves us without saying goodbye - dogs don't.

We abandon the path to scramble on slabs to the right of Craig Liathtais: slabs that are striped like bothy blankets. Bothy blankets? These are made in Harris Tweed factories from leftover wool. From a distance they're grey like the hills amongst which they are made, close up they contain every colour there is.

North-east of Creag Liathtais we go up the western extremity of the Cluanie Ridge on a path that twists among rocks: narrow, terraced on the steep bits for the ponies and marked at each corner with a compact cairn. This first one is Creag a' Mhaim but no one remembers the names of the Cluanies, just that there are seven of them all in a row.

As we climb, a lively wind plays around us. The day is now pale grey and luminous. These hills of the West are steep-sided and narrow with rocks all over the deep valleys between. Now we are poised at the end of one of these crests. It's two in the afternoon: as usual a bit later than we would like it to be. We see south to Glencoe; north to Applecross - about half of the Highlands. Far behind, the Corrieyairack looks like nothing in particular. There are three ridges ahead of us then no more; that's where Scotland stops.

We romp ahead over the seven Munros - Sir High was generous with them along here. Little bits of sea begin to appear among the hills on either

The South Cluanie Ridge: looking west over Sgurr An Lochain from Sgurr An Doire Leathain. One of the East-West ridges that are superhighways to (or from) the western shore. Loved by walkers for its grassy tops, plunging sides and occasional scrambles.   *Photo: Phil Iddon*

side and the ridge seems like a springboard that will take us forward and leave us several miles out to sea at a height of three thousand feet. It is the best of all ridges with short grass like meadow, enlivened with rocky bits. This real mountain ground is friendly too to the feet - after ten hours of it they feel better than they did after the first three miles of road.

Steep sided are these hills and carved sharp by interlocking glaciers. A Canadian on the Skye bus asked if Glen Shiel got many earthquakes. He assumed such sharp-edged mountains must still be heaving upwards.

Oddly the wind is boisterous in the bealachs (or *cols* to those who speak French) but gentle on the summits. It comes across the ridge from the southwest and, since it has to cross Ben Nevis to get here, we do not expect too much rain out of it. However we are getting rather tired.

"It's the walk of a lifetime," says the man on the fourth Cluanie, "I wish I was young enough."

People are nice but we don't tell him that we're already planning what walk of a lifetime to do next year.... over on the left there, the mysterious and tempting hills of Knoydart - Sgurr na Ciche, Ladhar Bheinn: they'll do for a start. On the right are the Affric Hills, where David and I got such a fine sunburn twenty years ago.

We reach the last Cluanie Hill, Craig nan Damh, at six-thirty. Ahead lie Sgurr na Sgine and the Saddle, whose famous Forcan Ridge it would be unwise to climb with these packs in this wind and as tired as this. Anyway we wouldn't get to Suardalan Bothy until after dark.

Quite by accident we bag a small Corbett with a big name, Sgurr a' Bhac Chaolais that lies in our way and spy a sheltered high corrie under Sgurr na Sgine and camp in it. We shall have to walk a bit extra tomorrow - that's all. You will choose your corrie according to the direction of the wind; this one at the head of Allt Coire Toiteal is excellent in a south-westerly.

I make a shelter for the cooker out of a large slab of stone. David's tent is indeed very small, but it's going to be a lot nicer than the Shelter Stone because it isn't raining and we aren't wet. We note the symmetry within the route of this and that earlier high bedroom. We are among craggy slopes on flat grass beside a stream, which is from a waterfall high overhead. The stone slab makes a good backrest. It's haggis and mash again; perhaps this is excess of symmetry but when we have a good idea we stick with it.

Some of the wind has found its way into our sheltered corrie. Is the tent going to blow down? Probably not, but if it does it doesn't weigh three million tons, which the Shelter Stone would be if it fell on you during the night. David's tent weighs 1.7 kg and he has carried it two-hundred miles for this occasion.

We set camp at eight, haggis ready at nine-thirty. David hasn't pre-measured his days but this incomplete one comes out at eighteen miles and 7500 feet so we're quite right to feel exhausted.

Foul weather alternative: To Glen Loyne and along it; over Bealach Coire Sgoireadail (try Skriddle) to Kinloch Hourn. There's a wood but no other accommodation that we could track down in Kinloch Hourn.

The Forcan Ridge of the Saddle. After so fine a summit you have to go and do six of the less interesting eastern Munros in compensation.   *Photo: Jim Teesdale*

DAY 12
Sgurr na Sgine to Glenelg
The famous Forcan Ridge
3300 feet 18 miles 8 1/2 hours

It rains in the night and is windy. David's tent is cosy but it does shrink when the gusts strike it. This alarms us for it's not that big to start with. Most of it is nine inches high, which I suppose is all you need when you're asleep. Even with a quarter of an hour lying and groaning we're up and away at seven-thirty, trying to catch up with ourselves after yesterday's shortcomings. Breakfast is porridge and honey sandwiches and it's just as well the rain stops at getting away time as I boiled over the porridge onto the tent's square yard of grass floored living area.

We lift on the sacks and thread between black, slimy rocks on sodden grass with little blue and yellow flowers in. It's the steepest available line to Sgurr na Sgine - this is David's way. Over the years we will become more rigorous in his demand for early starts, so that the first Munro at eight-thirty will seem positively laggardly. From the Beallach Coire Mhalagain it's a straight pull onto the Saddle but we decide to traverse right on a small path above a stone wall to the bottom end of the famous Forcan Ridge (948131).

The Forcan Ridge is not particularly difficult, but it has high, slabby sides to fall down and little rocky bits. It does go on being not particularly difficult to the trig. point on the Saddle's very summit. The little rocky bits are fine; it's the little narrow cols where the wind blows fiercely, that are frightening. David enjoys it. Then we go down westwards on another good ridge; this mountain doesn't have a gentle slope on it anywhere - well there is one small snowpatch just below the summit.

We leave the subsidiary Spidean by its SW ridge then NW to cross Druim na Firean. We continue on an up-and-down spur called Beinn Aoidhdailean to avoid having to descend the trackless valley with the same name, which is probably pronounced "ain". Somewhere there will be a Gaelic name in which every single letter is silent and which is pronounced simply " ".

When we look down at the trackless valley from its Beinn it has a huge path in it all the way down from its col. We join the path at 874144, which is where it starts on the map if not in real life - who are we to believe in Real Life where the map contradicts it?

All the bits of sea that we saw from the Cluanies have now disappeared behind us. The broad path takes us to a track, where we turn left for Glen Beag. It's a tight little valley where we look down on the tops of waving birch trees. Beside the track primroses and wild irises appear and we see a black and gold dragon fly. Further on is a Pictish fort built on a rock. Behind it a hundred foot bank of birch trees declines to the river; it's not hard to work out where they flung their rubbish. In the thickness of the wall there's a chamber eighteen inches wide and ten foot long. Low their standards of comfort may have been but nobody, nor even a hillwalker, could spend the night here unless imprisoned. Maybe they used it to keep their socks dry.

Lower down the valley are the two magnificent Brochs. A broch is a large circular building with no roof but very large walls. The walls are thick enough to have stairways and passages inside them, and a stack of triangular windows looking inwards over the door. David says that people who know what these things were for are wrong. The stonework is most attractive: huge blocks, four person lifters with finger-size slips filling between. The schist, or whatever it is, has good natural faces.

Along the tarmac road there's a bit of traffic. If the summer pastime of Fort Augustus is watching the boats go through the lochs, here it is driving

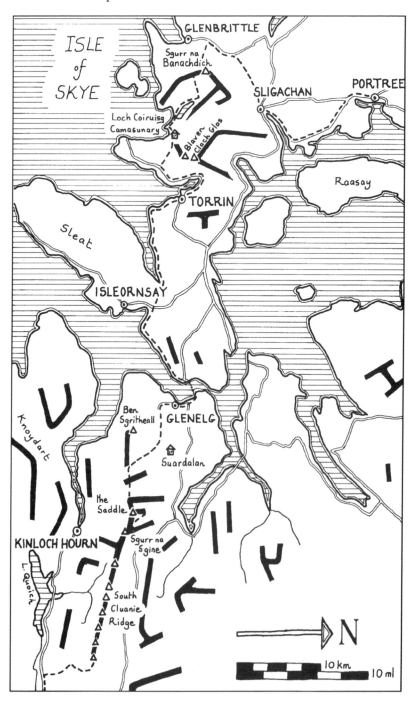

down to see the brochs. I think I can smell the sea now. Suddenly, there it is, round the back of a gorse bush.

We hit Glenelg at four and decide to stay rather than go on for 9.6 miles to Duisdale on Skye. We probably walk 9.6 miles discovering that all the B&B's are full. The tent on the beach or the Glenelg Hotel at £30 each? It's a lot to pay for a sock-wash and a bath but the hotel wins.

We share a table with a golfer/mother and a sailor/engineer. David has oysters and encourages me to have one too. I have soup - I always have soup; it's cheap calories, especially when you ask for extra bread. The oyster doesn't squirm on the way down. Ruth is having oysters too. She ordered them before but didn't dare eat them. She says they are tasty but poor value for money compared with whelks. Remembering our exit from Ballater we ask her if people are often killed by golf balls but she says golf balls do not travel fast enough to kill a person. The sailor/engineer says two modern bridges fell to bits and they had to go back to using General Wade's one and adds that the M6 through Birmingham should be OK now they've botched it back together again.

DAY 13
Glenelg to Torrin
Coast walking
27 miles 11 hours

Glenelg has a really nasty War Memorial. From a distance the soldier has a dismembered corpse with him but, close up, it is the naked female figure of Defeat crouched in an awkward posture. Over them hangs Victory - in massive bronze.

Again there's no breakfast before eight-thirty - that is the trouble with these classy places. We leave at nine-twenty past Bernera Barracks. This companion piece to Ruthven Barracks at Kingussie is a more interesting decay, with full-sized trees growing out of the masonry. It's handsome masonry too, but people have been mining it for corner stones. Now even the sign that says "keep away from the ruins" is in ruins.

Eyes now are on Skye across the narrow strip of blue-black water. The crossing of the mainland just completed is mere leg-loosening for the crossing of Skye to come. The leg-loosening has been effective; blisters are subdued and feet are eager along the road to the ferry, even as mind anxiously considers the rope at Duisdale, the Bad Step at Loch Scavaig, and the real possibility of failure on Sgurr na Banachdich.

The ferry has a turntable: they load cars on from the side and then two of them push the whole thing straight. David is impressed with the current through the narrows. "Nine knots", he says. A seal by the slipway dives and shows us her slippery back.

The map shows a path along the coast; this can mean the best walking of all if it exists or the worst if it doesn't. Here there is a path but it is small and keeps running away into the bog. So it's rough going. Splendid views across to the mainland compensate. David tells me everything he knows about the

Knoydart Peninsular over there. What David knows is that when the men came back from the Kaiser's War they threw out the landlords and declared a People's Soviet.

We thread along a hillside wood adorned with ancient holly and with streams running through. The path finally escapes into bog myrtle and we see rows of Christmas trees ahead. The map has the path striking boldly through the trees but Real Life doesn't seem to agree; a forest ride ahead has wheelmarks and wheelmarks must lead to a road. At the edge of the forest though, we are blocked by the gorge of Allt Thuill. Thuill is pronounced (and means) "hole". It is about fifty feet deep. We must head upstream to above the next waterfall, which we can hear but not see through the branches. Here the gorge is a bit shallower and a tiny path made by foxes leads surprisingly and quite excitingly down, across, up and out.

In the drama of crossing the gorge we lose track of our opening through the spruce and get a bad quarter of an hour among young trees. The way through them starts at the stream junction (GR 750167) and runs WSW. It'll be easier to find now these trees are big enough to define it. The gap becomes an alleyway through dense birch scrub, then a track, then the road. We want to turn right but first we must hide our sacks in the heather and trot down to the Duisdale Hotel to pick up David's rope. David's rope is quite heavy. I am NOT going to do the Thearlaich-Dubh Gap anyway.

We follow another path across a frightful bog: the latest map gives you a choice of two over the 25m altitude pass that is the neck of Sleat Peninsular, ours was the more northerly one. David's route plan called for us to swim the Abhainn Ceann Loch Eishort but it's not big enough for that and so we jump it rock-to-rock. We walk the tidemark of more rough coastline with fish farms and bits of drift-plastic tangled in wild iris. Heast is reached at five-thirty.

We cut the arc now over a moor of pink rocks, getting views over the sea from a bit higher up. A sea view should be half sea and half islands, blue-grey storm clouds and shafts of silver light bouncing on the water. When one of the islands has Rhum's crumpled outline, perfection is achieved.

Ahead there is another path-on-the-map. It gives us something to hope for in all these tussocks. Boreraig is an abandoned settlement with ruins, rabbits and a waterfall which crashes onto the beach. It was pulled down during the Clearances. Mackinnon, the hereditary piper of the Lord of the Isles, lived here. Now the hereditary piper has to fly in from Canada. It's written that the old people came back through the snow to die on their doorsteps.

The grass around the ruins is short like a lawn. A single slab big enough to roof a tomb acts as a footbridge and the start of our path. It leads under black cliffs and waterfalls. Evening thrushes sing out of the ivy that grows on rocks above. A rumble of thunder in Knoydart lasts for forty-three of my slowing paces. It rains a little and the midges rise, driving us forward. The path takes us up through a gap in the cliff along its top.

We round a curve of the coast. The clouds ahead have rocks in them. A steep hillside, higher in the air than it has a right to be, lifts out of one cloud and into another. On the right is Blaven, an impossibly pinnacled ridge and

Castles in the sky: Blaven seen across Loch Slapin

the start of the Black Cuillin range. At Suisnish the path becomes a track, then a road. The tarmac is speckled; the gravel in it is black gabbro and limestone from the Torrin Quarry.

David's research has failed us for there is no accommodation at Torrin and, though there is a post office, no shop. An old man sits on an old Fergie tractor beside the road. He seems midge-proof and his remaining teeth have the same basic outline as the pinnacles of Blaven. He thinks we may have passed a B&B a mile and a half back but we are too tired to return. We find enough breeze on the shore to keep away the midges and camp five-metres above the high water mark. David goes for water and comes back with a large tin of beans! "It was too big for me," the lady said: "I was going to give it to my daughter but you look as if you need it more." Beans and the emergency Kwik-Kook Nosh Risotto make an adequate supper.

DAY 14
Torrin to Glen Brittle
Crossing the Cuillin
20 miles 4200 feet 13 hours

The flysheet is translucent; we can see all the midges on the outside waiting for their breakfast. We have a quick one of our own - sandwiches and water - and move off sharply at seven. This little tent is great for early starts. We go round the head of Loch Slapin and up the track from Kilmarie to Camasunary. The road is hard but the track is a stony delight, especially when the vertical wilderness of the Cuillin rises up over the pass.

For the really enterprising, the crossing to Camasunary by Sgurr nan Each, Clach Glas and Blaven (named Bla Bheinn on the latest maps) is one of Scotland's greatest mountain days - but you will need good nerves and a rope for the ridge of Clach Glas, a rock climb graded moderate. I notice that Clach Glas (GR 534221) is not named on the O.S. Landranger map; it is too low for a Munro, and hasn't enough drop for Corbett's Table, though more than enough for anyone else with two thousand foot sheer fall on both sides of the ridge.

We take two hours to reach Camasunary Bothy, which is set in a lovely bay with grey sand beaches and green meadow. Here we eat another breakfast - one of porridge and soup - and peer through the windows at the black, mist-topped mountains ahead. The footbridge beyond the bothy seems to have burnt down but this will not present problems except when the river's full and the tide is in. The problem I am worrying about is the "Bad Step", a hard move along this coastal path to Coiruisg. Iron-grey boiler-plates slope down to the sea and the path squelches through much black bog. The sea is turquoise over sand and dark over rock. The Bad Step is perfectly easy, clambering over gently angled rocks with large holds. Leap suddenly sideways off those hand holds, though and you do fall fifty feet into the sea. The rock is rough Cuillin gabbro: a foot on it at any angle will hold. Some reassurance: the scrambling over Sgurr na Banachdich is no harder than Bad Step.

The Cairngorms and the Cuillin are the two outstanding Scottish ranges but, where the Cairngorms are rounded and huge, the Cuillin are jagged - very jagged. Although Loch Coiruisg is fifty feet above sea level and Loch Avon is 2500 feet higher, the two situations correspond rather closely. There's no easy way out except the way we came in. David's idea, and the reason he brought the rope, is that we should get out by the truly difficult and demanding route, "Doing the Dubhs". This not only sounds good (the pronunciation of Dubh sounds the same as do), but it is good. It contains several miles of rock-climbing over Sgurr Dubh Beag, Sgurr Dubh Mor, Sgurr Dubh na Da Bheinn (Skurr Doona Darven) and three peaks of the main ridge to get to Sgurr na Banachdich. An awe-inspiring day's mountaineering: this would make the journey so far seem like a walk in the park but, with the cloud down on the tops, wet rock, and the fact that it's nearly lunchtime already, we don't even stop to think about it. Just as well: I am NOT capable of the Thearlaich-Dubh gap, whatever David says.

The stepping stones at the foot of Loch Coiruisg will be under water if it's been raining a lot. In that case you'll use the path up the east side of the loch, otherwise the western one is slightly less harsh.

Coiruisg means "Corrie of the Waters" and there's a lot of the stuff about. Black crags with streams splashing down them hang over three sides and the sky gets smaller as we enter. At the foot of the loch, two hundred yards from the sea, it is sunny with white, fluffy clouds, but at its head grey mist is low and fierce gusts of wind blow round and round in the hollow. Breaking out of this circle of dark cliffs that run up to the cloud is an intimidating prospect.

The going along the valley floor is heavy - rocks and bog. It feels like uphill but, as we are going alongside the loch, it cannot be so. A mile in from the lake we turn left to climb beside a cascading stream. Above us, on our left, the rock prow of Sgurr Coir' an Lochain is like an icebreaker bashing through the mist. The climb is steep and at fifteen hundred feet the stream becomes a waterfall, pounding over slabs of rock. We move left to avoid the slabs and up a steep boulder-field until we can move right again to the stream. The slope relents for a short way and we are walking on a sparsely-cairned track across vegetation. We are two thousand feet up, the altimeter says, and well into the cloud. The faint path leads along the base of the screes of Sgurr Dearg (which are on our left) and then goes up them. It's a frightfully steep slope - the roughness of gabbro is a disadvantage here for it means that Cuillin screes lie steeper. After seven hundred feet of hard work a rock wall appears on the left. Stonecrops grow in it - plumper and more healthy than the ones in my garden. Although our feet are still on the scree the rock offers stationary handholds. Another wall appears on the right and we are climbing in a gully.

The pass on the ridge is five feet wide, rock on both sides and with more screes plunging down beyond. The wind, and there's a good deal of it, is at right-angles to the one down at the loch. This is Bealach Coire na Banachdich. It's three-thirty in the afternoon and we must now find Sgurr na Banachdich. This is tricky. The Cuillin is mostly rock and a wrong turn will leave us trapped among the cliffs. Ordinary maps do not work; everything's so steep they cannot draw the contour lines. Worse still, the compass doesn't work very well - the rocks are magnetic! I have with me an altimeter, which is never needed on lesser hills. We follow the verbal description in the guide book - but words lack the descriptive power of maps - and scratchmarks on the rock. Too high and the rock-scrambling becomes difficult; too low and we lose touch with the ridge-crest. After half an hour another party scrambles towards us out of the cloud.

"Have you seen Sgurr na Banachdich?" we ask.

"Oh it's back there, fifty metres away."

This is clearly impossible. They are pointing downhill. We decide that we must have missed the summit by traversing below it and climb back up the ridge-crest. We find a summit but it does not match the description "at the far end of a small summit plateau the cairn is poised over a small abyss." There's abyss everywhere in the mist but no plateau, just five feet of flat bit. However the time to reach it and the depth of the dip in the ridge beyond it mean that it has to be the right one. The altimeter disagrees; we still have twenty metres to go. Oh well. We take an orange, a Mars bar and a summit photo and I deposit my lump of granite from Mount Keen. A geologist should recognize this at once and deduce a most easterly to most westerly Munro walk. Will lumps of black gabbro now appear on Mount Keen?

We come across the other party starting down a blind gully on the Coiruisg (that is the wrong) side of the ridge. We are rather lost but they are completely lost. I find myself asking them pertinent questions. "Does someone expect you back? Do they know your route?" Because we are not absolutely certain we are on Banachdich summit we shall not look for the direct route but return to Bealach Coire na Banachdich, where we came up, and descend the other side. In clear conditions there's a straightforward path down the west ridge of Sgurr na Banachdich, or you could continue over

Sgurr na Banachdich the second of the Two Tops and a typical more interesting Western Munro. Seen across Bealach Coire na Banachdich with Sgurr Thormaid behind. The Two Tops route takes the ridge from Bealach Coire na Banachdich to the summit.

Sgurr Ghreadaidh northwards, even as far as Sgurr a Mhadaidh - it's all real ridge but no rock-climbing.

We offer to take the lost party. They are slow; all are tired and two are just starting to get frightened. I seek out the route and David, his glasses all misted up, is reassuring at the back. He quickly dispels the mood of anxiety. (Well I'm anxious, but hiding it.) Our rope is out of sight in the sack and we decide to keep quiet about it; with a rope on, the speed of the party will drop to something indistinguishable from zero. We reach the Beallach quite slowly but without difficulty, helped by a couple of momentary clearances in the mist. We've been just two hours on the ridge but it feels longer.

We say goodbye and head off joyfully down the scree, relieved to be moving at full speed again. A minute later we say hello again; the scree has led us to the top of a vertical gully. "Damn," says David "I've seen this before." This turns out to be the place where he got lost last time he was here. Casting up and down the hill we find some wrong cairns - wicked, that - and some right ones. It is necessary to keep hard left under the rocks for quite a way at the start of this descent. By rejecting all difficult ground, we get down out of the mist and onto slopes that are just ordinarily steep.

"Thanks very much," says Brian. "Where are you staying? Can we give you a lift somewhere? Come to our cottage and have wine, whisky and a big meal." We explain that we're not staying, just passing through, and the ethical necessity of walking towards Portree. They agree to pick us up at Sligachan at eight.

This is impossible. Even they, with a car at the bottom of the hill, will not be at Sligachan by eight. We gallop down alongside the gorge with a

Reichenbachian one hundred foot waterfall. David reveals that he has never heard of Kylie Minogue - what sheltered lives some people lead. Full of energy, we stride up the road. There's a path in two and a half miles where we'll turn off for Sligachan, which we will reach not at eight but at ten. The shop will be shut and we ate our emergency food this morning.

It will be rather convenient if Brian's party catch up with us on the road, take us to Carbost and re-deposit us at the same point in the morning. We walk and walk. Four cars pass, of which two offer us lifts, and we reach the path turn-off. We delay, eating chocolate.

David, who has already started on the path, says, "There's one coming." It is them.

We're whisked off to Carbost for a very large meal with lots of good wine. They press on us second and third helpings and exclaim in horror over David's feet. Brian is laughed at for throwing his rucksack into the Mad Burn during their crossing of the Shore Path the day before. (They had camped at Coiruisg.) He hadn't wanted to throw too hard in case he did his back in. The sack sailed down the river like a slalom canoe.

David and I go to bed on the living room floor. We've decided that the walk may end in Portree - our original intention had been Rubha Hunish, the northernmost tip of Skye. Stonehaven to Portree is one fishing village to another. Also David must get home for the London to Brighton Cycle Rally.

Foul weather alternative: To Coiruisg as before, then the Shore Path to Glenbrittle.

There's one problem with that: the Mad Burn (Allt a Chaoich). The catchment of this stream is entirely bare rock and two hours after it starts raining it can quite suddenly become a vertical river. Wait, or head out to Sligachan by the well-marked path north past Loch a Choire Riabhaich. If the Mad Burn can be crossed then the shore path climbs SW from the burn's foot to about the 300m contour, then follows this round. Eventually the path that descends from Coir' a Ghrunnda is joined and followed down to Glenbrittle Camp Site. On these low slopes your compass will not mislead you.

DAY 15
Glen Brittle to Portree
14 miles 1000 feet 7 hours

"England will declare at 240 for 6 in their second innings," Steve predicted confidently. "Man of the match will not be an Australian but Alan Lamb, for saving the draw for England." The news this morning informs us however that England have lost disastrously. Brian drives us back while the others breakfast on toast with peanut butter, pickle and marmite - all on the same slice.

It is a lovely, sunny day with not a cloud on the Cuillin. Mountains are often compared with castle walls but the Cuillin really is a great rampart around Coiruisg. I will be back again to knock on those iron-grey gates but next time I'll get to know the main passes and ways off before trying any big chunks of the ridge.

The path over the Bealach a' Mhaim goes down beside another Skye gorge with small waterfalls to Sligachan. We get an excellent pub lunch at the Sligachan Hotel. For over a century climbers have been peering in contemplation over their beers from this place back to the Cuillin skyline.

Although David must go home for his cycle race I plan a fast traverse of Trotternish to get back to Portree the same night and maybe even the Skye Half Marathon on Saturday. In this aspiration I am encouraged by a misleading weather forecast pinned up in the bar. Skye is notorious for its misleading weather.

Out of Sligachan ("the Bay of Shells") we take the coast path north westwards. It is a beautiful one with views across the sea but it is not remote for the only two way road on Skye is across the loch. Eight miles of pleasant road take us through little villages called the Braes. In the celebrated 'Battle of the Braes' of 1882 the local crofters resisted the bailiffs who had come to evict them - and won. As a result these villages are prosperous and alive, whilst only the rabbits run over Boreraig.

Cool breeze and warm sunlight on Skye: a pleasantly idented coastline with the woods and rocks of Raasay opposite: why then are we so listless? It's because we're walking away from the Cuillin. After such a noble crossing, mere flat road has to be an anti-climax.

Anti-climax though is no excuse for going past Ben Tianavaig on the road. The proper end must be to climb this striking small hill with, in the sack, two bottles from the Sligachan Inn. (They call it Sligachan Ale but in fact its the good Greenmantle from the Borders.)

Portree is warm and pink in the evening light. Pinkest of all is the Pink Guest House, which overlooks the harbour just like the Marine Hotel in Stonehaven. Run by an amiable camp couple, it's as pink inside as out and with a fishtank in the lounge.

DAY 16
Portree to Portree

I rise at two and set out at three-thirty for my rapid transit to Rubha Hunish thirty-five miles away. I start well, moving fast in my trainers under the street lights. At 1500 feet on Beinn a' Chearcaill I meet mist and driving rain and discover that the magnetic rocks are here too, playing tricks with my compass. The situation is dodgy for a lone walker. On the right are twenty miles of cliff, on the left an awful lot of moor. Certainly there will be no fast crossing today.

Steering by the wind, I return to Portree, which is full of midges in the drizzle. Fortunately, at six in the morning the front door of the Pink House is not locked. David is still asleep. I have another bath. Oh well, we did agree Portree was a valid endpoint.

During the walk David has unravelled the mysteries of Naming Theory. This is something in psycholinguistics. So - a productive fortnight.

DATA FILE

Our Schedule

Section	distance miles	ascent (ft)	time hours
1 Stonehaven - Auchenblae	15½	700	8
2 Auchenblae - Tarfside	22	2500	9½
3 Tarfside - Ballater	21	2600	8
4 Ballater - Cock Bridge	14	3300	8
5 Cock Bridge - Shelter Stone	23	5500	10
6 Shelter Stone - Kingussie	26	5500	12½
7 Kingussie - Laggan Bridge	15	600	8
8 Laggan Bridge - Ft Augustus	26	1400	10
9 Rest day			
10 Ft Augustus - Tomdoun	19	800	8
11 Tomdoun - Sgurr na Sgine	18	7500	10¾
12 Sgurr na Sgine - Glenelg	18	3300	8½
13 Glenelg - Torrin	27	0	11
14 Torrin - Glen Brittle	20	4200	13
15 Glen Brittle - Portree	14	1000	7
Total	275	40000	132
Daily average	20	2800	9½

ACCOMMODATION

Selected Hotels

Stonehaven	Marine Hotel, 9/10 Shore Road	62806
Cock Bridge	Allargue Arms	Strathdon 51410
Laggan	Monadliath Hotel	276/308
Tomdoun	Tomdoun Hotel (bunkhouse)	218
Sligachan	Sligachan Inn (bunkhouse)	650204
Portree	Pink Guest House, Quay Street	612263

Youth Hostels
Ballater 55227, Kingussie 661506, Glenbrittle (full: must be booked) Carbost 640278

Bothies

Glen Dye	Charr Bothy
Glen Tanar	Shiel of Glentanar
Glenavon	Faindouran Lodge
	Fords of Avon (inaccessible when river in spate)
Loch Avon	Shelter Stone
Coire Etchachan	Hutchison Memorial Hut
Lairig Ghru	Corrour bothy - can be crowded and squalid
	Garbh Coire Bothy - very small
Glen Feshie	Ruigh Aiteachain Bothy (Island House) - a nice one with some firewood
Glen More	Suardalan Bothy at GR 883173
Skye	Camasunary - idyllic site but heavily used
	Coiruisg - JMCS Hut: members only: must be booked

Crucial Shops
Glen Esk (one small shop), Laggan (tel. 257), Invergarry, Isle Ornsay (3 miles off route), Glenbrittle (Campsite shop), Sligachan (Campsite shop tel. 650303)

Best Restaurant in Scotland
Kingussie   The Cross, Tweed Mill Brae Tel 661166

Tourist Information Centres

Aberdeen	632727
Stonehaven	62806
Ballater	55306
Braemar	41600
Kingussie	661297
Fort Augustus	6367
Portree	612137

Afterword to Chapter Two
On Scottish Ranges beginning with "C"

You can get a blizzard in the Cairngorms on any day of the year; the ones in summer do not last for more than a day. The best way to risk death is by getting lost for exhaustion and hypothermia will soon follow. It is rather easy to get lost in an unexpected whiteout when your fingers are too cold to hold the compass and the map is blowing apart.

The Cairngorms are different to other ranges. Do not be scared, but do be respectful. Carry not one but two extra layers of clothing and put those layers on before you ascend into the snowstorm; there are few sheltered spots on the plateau. Memorize in advance the 'desperation bearing' that will get you off the plateau without having to steer round the tops of any cliffs - even if it does take you into Braemar when you wanted Glen Feshie. Steer by the wind as well as the compass; you can check the wind without taking your hands out of your pockets. Be prepared to admit that the Cairngorms are bigger than you - they are!

I thought I could find my way off anywhere in Scotland; take out a map, find a ridge and go down it on a compass bearing until out of the cloud. Not in the Cuillin. There is so much happening that the map is illegible; the compass doesn't work either, and the ridge becomes a precipice half way down. Glencoe and the Torridons are, let's face it, dirt with plants growing out of it but the Cuillins are all mountain. Even things ordinary hills have, like weather, like bogs and like midges, Skye has more of.

This year I returned to the bit between the Bealach and the Sgurr na Banachdich. It wasn't cloudy, the rock was dry, the ridge was obvious and my hand touched rock about twice on the whole section....but in 1988 we wondered whether to get out the rope.

On Skye, and nowhere else, I walk with a guidebook. On Skye, and nowhere else, I walk with an altimeter. Do not ignore the compass - it's close most of the time. Again the wind can be used for direction. Most of all, examine the ground. Generations of Scottish Mountaineering Club members have been along the main ridge, marking the holds with their hobnails. The difference between scree that has been trodden on and scree that hasn't is plain, once you look for the signs.

Chapter Three
SUMMITS of the SOUTH
Oban to Arbroath
A High-level Route Over 43 Munros

In the Summer of 1990 I wrote to David pointing out that we were going to reach the age of forty in early 1991 and offering as a birthday treat a choice of forty-mile walks. I suggested a Dartmoor and Exmoor Coast to Coast and the Galloway 2000 footers. His response was an entry form to the 1991 Ultimate Challenge. I agreed, with the proviso that, since the Ultimate Challenge is not ultimately challenging (deriving its name from its then sponsors, Ultimate Equipment), we should mark the anniversaries by including at least forty Munro summits in the crossing.

In order to gain the 40-odd summits with not too much horizontal stuff in between I mapped out an extreme southerly route, starting at Oban and finishing at Auchmithie, which is a little fishing village near Arbroath and home of the Arbroath smokie. This offered a fair number of seldom-trod unglamorous peaks that followed one after another. David accepted this on the grounds that it was a very different route to any he would have chosen.

The result is seriously energetic in the terms of ups and downs. The hills are, however, less terrifying than those on the Two Tops walk; they are near the pleasant end of the pleasant-exciting-frightening spectrum. Much of the going is high-altitude stroll and civilization is never more than half a day's walk away. If I have a reservation about the route it is that it is too easy: even the route-finding is easy. The only place we got lost was on a forest road above Loch Tummel. In this chapter, therefore, I have decided to offer a more wide and generous style of route description - one with space inside it to wander around.

The Foul Weather Alternatives, linked together, give a rather fine low-level crossing by a succession of lonely valleys and high passes. Only six miles of Glen Lochay and, of course, the tramp out to the east coast is on the road.

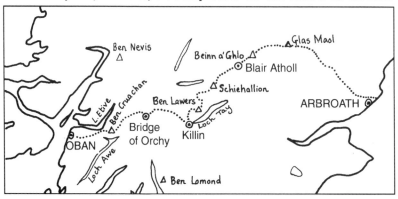

An odd feature of this crossing is that it can be embellished with the ascent of no fewer than 16 Corbetts. Perhaps it's a high-level-after-all.

DAY 0
Taynuilt

May 9th was a lovely Spring day spent on the train. Taynuilt is an attractive pierhead village with real beer (light, heavy and severe) brewed on the premises in the station waiting room. Tomorrow night there will be real music too. The bar has pictures of crashed trains and a dead longhorn steer and pictures of bar regulars fooling around on the summit of Cruachan. It looks good up there.

I have stopped here so that we may leave our luggage and do our first day (Oban to Taynuilt) unladen. I do a brief recce in the evening light. The paths we shall take are prickly and scented: gorse into Taynuilt, hawthorn out. Shall we make 40 summits? Barring bad weather, bad legs, yes; but they are both quite likely. A sweepstake then: how many? I'll say 38. I had toned down our route plan for the Ultimate Challenge vetters. Even so the vetters thought it a bit much. "You may have more fun if you attempt less," they wrote, but admitted that they had recently reached forty themselves.

I study the map and choose a wood a mile or two out of town in which to sleep. No tent yet: David's bringing it in the morning. It is a pleasant night - starry and rather cold, with much dew towards the morning. There are views along Loch Etive. You get the full benefit of these things in a bivvi bag as you do not sleep that much. Cruachan looks big from here, with cloud rising off and a few snow-streaks.

DAY 1
Oban to Taynuilt
17½ mile, 1800 feet: 6¼ hours

It is pleasing when complicated arrangements actually work. David leapt off the train clutching not only his own rucksack but another, thrust into his arms by a total stranger who spotted his chance to walk unladen too. We left the rucksack at Mrs Diggory's and took the bus to Oban.

Gazing out to Mull we think it's a shame the UC rules forbid us to start on Iona and come in over Ben More. The hordes of the ultimately challenged are here somewhere but Oban also contains greater hordes of ordinary humans. We leave through shopping streets that become a narrow tarmac road, which winds amongst crags and golf courses even before the thirty mile an hour limit ends.

After meeting some 'lowland challengers' we dodge (at Muircroft) into a forest with more tracks than are shown on the map. Thus tarmac and fellow humans are avoided to the lonely Loch Nell. Here we are to climb Beinn Ghlas (1830ft), both to avoid more tarmac and to show we are not mere Munro-baggers....

Beinn Ghlas looks on the map like a boggy hump but turns out better, with no bogs but little crags and fine backward views - half mountain and half sea.

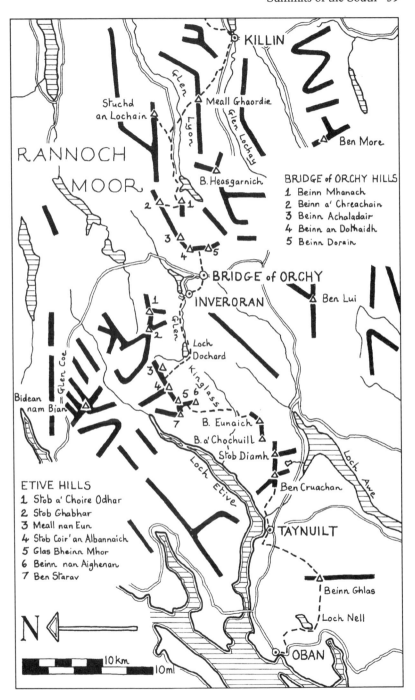

KILLIN

Glen Lyon

Stuchd an Lochain

Meall Ghaordie

Glen Lochay

RANNOCH

MOOR

Ben More

B. Heasgarnich

BRIDGE of ORCHY HILLS
1 Beinn Mhanach
2 Beinn a' Chreachain
3 Beinn Achaladair
4 Beinn an Dothaidh
5 Beinn Dorain

BRIDGE of ORCHY

INVERORAN

Ben Lui

Glen

Loch Dochard

Kinglass

Bidean nam Bian

Glen Coe

B. Eunaich

B. a' Chochuill

Stob Diamh

Loch Etive

Ben Cruachan

Loch Awe

ETIVE HILLS
1 Stob a' Choire Odhar
2 Stob Ghabhar
3 Meall nan Eun
4 Stob Coir' an Albannaich
5 Glas Bheinn Mhor
6 Beinn nan Aighenan
7 Ben Starav

TAYNUILT

N

Beinn Ghlas

Loch Nell

10km
10ml

OBAN

We climb it beside the Eas Criche, a lovely lunch-spot between rocks and water with little bog-flowers. No lay-by on the Glen Lonan road boasts these features. There are many rocky tops and it's hard to find the highest. A bit of a track, then some road, take us down to Airds Bay on the shores of Loch Etive.

It wouldn't do at all to enter Tainuilt like a motorist along the A85(T). The path along Loch Etive and beside the River Nant is the main road into the village for those who like their hills upside-down in sea water.

We come into Tainuilt though gorse, primroses, wood anenomes and so on. It has been an undemanding day given that the first day out is always demanding. Tomorrow, at least we'll have a good excuse for being demanded upon.

There's no live music after all but half a dozen live 'Challenged' in the station platform pub. Frank gets his rucksack back from David; the Challenged require no prearranged rendezvous in a village with its own brewery. Frank is proud of his OAP bus pass and once cycled from Wanlockhead to Cockermouth in a single day in 1949. He tries to persuade us all to spend a jolly night together in a container lorry he spotted two miles up the path four weeks ago. No takers. Disgusted, he turns away to chat up some women who still have thirty years to wait for their own bus passes. In no time at all they are all having a good laugh about Kirkintilloch and remembering each other to their grandmothers.

Another of the Challenged has an arm swollen beneath his rucksack. It has become inert and tingling. We all think the arm is going to drop off but are too polite to say so.

In the B&B David rabbits on about his new baby and her fascinating nappies. I haven't told him yet about my own daughter Jessie's big win in the colouring-in competition. David's rucksack turns out to weigh 37lb - ugh! This includes the tent, kitchenware and food for three days as well as two torches and a book (Lord Jim). Mine is 22lb until he puts many of the aforementioned into it. The total is still small by UC standards. David met a man with 45lb, including a big bottle of whisky and the longest ice-axe he's ever seen.

DAY 2
Taynuilt to Glen Kinglass
Ben Cruachan (4 summits)
16 miles, 8200 feet; 10½ hours

There are Frieslanders in our B&B. They say it's so flat in Friesland that you look out of the window on Sunday and see who's coming to visit on Wednesday, which is why they have come to Scotland. It is a reasonable looking day with a bit of cloud on the tops. Everybody says that it is going to rain like anything the night after next, which is when we camp high in the Etives.

We cross the River Awe on a dangling footbridge of cathedral proportions. A route-finding error dumps us in a birchwood which David finds delightful: it was David's route-finding error. Another error - a track on the right, not

David (right) and myself on Ben Cruachan   Photo: David Howard

marked on the map - leads by sheer luck to a path right up through the Christmas trees to the open slopes of Coire Seilich, which lies beneath Meall nan Each.

Ben Cruachan was once thought to be the highest mountain in Scotland, but not by us as we start to ascend a vast grassy slope three miles wide and three thousand feet high. The adjusted rucksack is heavy but comfortable. I had it fine-tuned at Graham Tiso's shop on the way through Glasgow. Soon all the fields and moorland are a pretty pattern spread out below and nothing to do with us any more.

The Nordend of Monte Rosa has been called 'the Taynuilt peak of Switzerland'. Certainly there's a steep fierce bit with large rocks and snow patches. The hills are said to be snowier this year, which is a bit worrying because we have no axes. From Tainuilt Peak (unnamed: 1101m) to the main summit is a ridge of granite lumps. The main peak leans over its northern corrie to give that pointy silhouette that makes Cruachan such an easy one to spot from Ben Nevis. The ridge, however, just clambers amiably over the lumps, while cloud comes and goes, showing hundreds of mountains in every direction.

Cruachan is two morning Munros and the 1300 foot climb for the two in the afternoon is taken slowly but with some determination. Our slow start has paid off and we are going well over Beinns a' Chochuill and Eunaich, which are pleasant grassy ones where sheep may safely graze and, in fact, do. Four climbed, thirty-nine to go. In the 'how many Munros' sweepstake David puts his money on forty-two.

The route plan says we must cross the hump of Meall Copagach. What nonsense we say and, without looking at the map (who needs it when you can see fifty miles in all directions?), traverse down into the only craggy bit on the whole slope. We don't deserve them but a series of rocky shelves lets us through and down into Glen Kinglass. Here the birds are tweeting and the trees are coming into leaf. We go an extra two miles into Allt Hallater because Hamish Brown did and there might be wind in the main valley. It's a birch-hung gorge - one of those where Scotland pays a passing tribute to Tibet. The ground consists of rocks, drumlins, pools, all in glacier-shredded chunks with the sound of waterfalls in nearby chasms. We climb nearly a thousand feet to find a flat bit.

The flat bit we find is beside a stream that splashes down green granite slabs and greener pools. David strips naked to wash. He is becoming more and more eccentric with age. Nakedness is entirely appropriate on these bare slopes but washing only one dayout from a B&B? The haggis is as good as ever and washing up in the waterfall is rather exciting; what if I drop a spoon? OK, we do have a spare.

Foul Weather Alternative: from Inverawe House take the track alongside Loch Etive and Glen Kinglass. The Inveroran Hotel is reached by way of 22 miles of track and path. Three assorted Corbetts between Glen Srae and Lochy are a tougher way to get to the Bridge of Orchy.

DAY 3
Glen Kinglass to Inveroran
Beinn nan Aighenan, Glas Bheinn Mhor,
Stob Coir' an Albannaich
16½miles 5000 ft; 9 hours

David wakes me at six, singing hymns. He enunciates his First Law:

> "Because it isn't raining we must get up quickly before it is. At once it does and, in fact, this day turns into a very nasty one but all the same we do get our three summits and a hot shower."

It's a rain that increases sneakily with no sudden gust that says, "stop now, remove waterproofs and put more warm things underneath". By the time we get to the ridge we're in cloud with driving rain - too nasty to even consider removing outer clothing. It was to drive nastier as the day unfolded. A good stalkers' path leads us up the valley among little pools, through gorges and into cloud. Horse dung on it shows that it is still used to carry down dead deer. Hamish Brown left his rucksack at the bottom of Beinn nan Aighenan's north ridge so we do too. Even without being able to see it, we can tell that this is a fine mountain by its chunkiness underfoot and the raindrops that blow sideways off its many rocks.

Don't you think people look silly with those plastic map cases dangling around their necks? I do too. Here on Beinn nan Aighenan the wind plucked the flapping uncased map from my cold fingers. I got it back - all but one unimportant corner that flew away as if seeking mystic union with the piece of land it images. A Platonist, clearly, this map fragment: aware that it and the land alike are mere illegal photocopies of the (non-existent and so ultimately real) Idea of Map.

David has an altimeter in his watch. Is it a gimmick? Certainly it does make it very easy to find the sacks again. We decide to omit Ben Starav since it is quite invisible and, anyway, only one of our optional extras. On Glas Bheinn Mhor the ridges are steep and bouldery: steep and bouldery enough to be enjoyable, even with water running down the back of the neck. We climb the next one, the one with the Gaelic name meaning the Scotsman (Stob Coir' an Albannaich). By this time it's no longer possible, even for us, perverse as we are, to persuade ourselves we're still having fun. We don't want to do things along this ridge for six hours and then go to sleep on it; we want off and we want off now.

There's a difficulty here. Leaving the Scotsman requires some complicated map reading through the various craggy bits that make this such a worthwhile hill. Even the smallest amount of map-reading is going to lead to the disintegration of our map. I decide that we should return to the col we just left. David decides that we should go forward not back as back is into the wind and the wet stuff. However, I am the one with the map.

David is quite right about the wet stuff. It comes in through the hood opening and goes out again at the ankles.

We go down Eas a' Choire Dhuibhe into the wild grandeur of a stormswept glen, through splashing rills and springing burns. We cross jolly big rivers where there shouldn't be jolly big rivers but our feet don't get any wetter than they are already. Our foul-weather fallback is the stable at Loch Dochard. Once we reach its sheltering walls we do what we should have done five hours ago: take off our waterproofs and several wet layers beneath to insert warm thermal bits and pieces. Only then do we look around us.

The foul-weather fallback at Loch Dochard really is foul. It has some roof but not much; windows with real wind though and a soaking wet cobblestone floor only slightly softened by the layer of litter. Sad stories of the children of the Duke of Edinburgh are scrawled on the wall. One wrote of waking to find the loch inside his tent and wading out thigh-deep in the dark with all his belongings on his head.

With a single voice we reject this poor, lowly stable as well as the three unclaimed summits along the ridge. We head for the oldest inn in the Highlands, the Inveroran Hotel (1780), which is six miles down the path and also falling to bits. (Take the riverside path not the track by Clashgour.)

As we enter the bar at six it suddenly becomes a lovely day. According to UC control it's going to a beautiful day all night and start raining again in the morning. Our room is quickly draped with damp objects such as the tent, David and me. We have a bar snack followed by a bar supper and wash several pairs of socks.

Fair Weather Alternative: Meall nan Eun, Stob Gabhar. The south ridge of Stob Gabhar gives a comfortable descent to Forest Lodge; Aonach Eagach is an interesting alternative. Best of all is to continue over Stob a' Choire Odhair then down the SW ridge of Beinn Toaig.

DAY 4
Glen Orchy to Glen Lyon
Beinns Dorain, an Dothaidh,
Achaladair, a' Chreachain and Mhanach
21 miles, 8000 feet; 11½hours

It was indeed fine all night and raining pretty hard by morning. I complimented the seventy-year-old chef on his real porridge and he told me in detail how to make it the way I do anyway:

Real Porridge (per person)
small cup of medium oatmeal (NOT porridge oats)
3½ same-size cups of water
salt

Soak the oatmeal in half the water overnight. In the morning add the rest of the water, bring to the boil, stirring and cook for five minutes. Serve with salt for authenticity though I like mine with golden syrup.

There's a blind Alsatian dog staying here too. It's doing the West Highland Way except that it has to go on the main road from time to time to avoid the lambing fields. We are now a day ahead and three miles and three hills behind: seven climbed, thirty-three to go. With grim determination we set out to do the next four hills in the rain and low cloud. We take various precautions that were omitted yesterday like putting waterproofs on before starting to get wet and doing all the bearings and altitudes on a bit of paper in a plastic bag.

We start down a bit of West Highland Way: it's a military road with lots of culverts and a good, hard footing so that the many feet have only made bog here and there. The way ambles gently up the hillside with fine views of Ben Dorain and Ben More - fortunately these views are printed on the official guide since they are not visible though the cloud. We pass thirty-two walkers on this two and a half mile section, including a party of seventeen draped with plastic carrier-bags.

At Bridge of Orchy (warning - no shop) we collect our food parcel from the hotel. The bulgar wheat, substituting for bread, has leaked and so has the marmalade. Since we are a day ahead of schedule we have too much food and so we abandon the bulgar along with the packaging into which it has integrated itself. David points out that there would have been no way to spread the marmalade on the bulgar anyway though the reverse process of spreading the bulgar on the marmalade might just about be feasible.

We climb Beinn Dorain up a mixture of 50% black squelch and 50% rainwater. Beinn Dorain is where the Ripleys gave up. The Ripleys attempted all 277 Munros in one walk and fell prey to bad weather (they started in August), bad diet (no vitamins, too few calories) and demoralization. With only forty left they told themselves, "If we can do Beinn Dorain we can do the rest." They could not. The nice man on breakfast TV has promised and

I, in turn, have promised all the wet West Highland Wayfarers, that the rain is going to stop by three. At two o' clock the clouds flap away like sheets from a sodden clothes-line. We see the hillsides streaked with fresh waterfalls and snow. We get dry. I claim this as a reward from the gods for having carried out a small bag

Ben Dorain

of rubbish from the nasty stable. David claims it as vindication of his Second Law:

> "When it's raining, get onto the hill as early as possible. Then if it gets better you're up there already; and, if it gets worse, you've taken advantage of the best part of the day."

Dothaidh is pronounced "dough". After the Etives, its craggy slopes are kindly for between the crags is short grass with a little path up it. The clouds go away altogether and the views spread out in all directions - back two days to Cruachan, forward two more to Ben Lawers. We find ourselves on a high shelf, looking down like ornamental plaster dogs on the bumps and puddles of Rannoch Moor. With the grins of ornamental plaster dogs we pass over Beinn Achaladair. Beinn Achaladair is where Grandpa fell through the cornice. He and my father had been looking for a way down off the shelf. My father turned to say "this could be it" and saw footprints leading to a broken edge of snow. It was only a small cornice, about eighteen inches, but that was enough for Grandpa. There's a small buttress halfway down and he took it like a ski jump. He broke his arm and was lucky not to lose an ear as well as his car-keys. Luckily this was in the days when the AA could start your car with a piece of copper wire. He was a proper mountaineer, my Grandpa, and not a mere long-distance desperado like his descendant but even small cornices are dangerous.

Today the cornice is even smaller and neither of us falls through. We take in Beinn Mhanach, an optional extra, in a fit of enthusiasm. This means back-tracking from Creachain to the head of Glen Cailliche and leaving rucksacks near 364425.

On Beinn Mhanach all the authorities mention this: "it's got something to do with monks". Perhaps that is because there's nothing else to say. It's a fea-tureless lump just over three thousand feet high and a long where from anywhere. I persuade David that he wants to do it to save having to trudge here in thirty year's time on his last Munros thinking "I was right here in 1991, when I was only 40 and didn't do it."

On the way down we get some snow runs in a little gully. A fair-sized stream goes under the snow at the top and comes out at the bottom so we know it's under there somewhere; this makes it all quite exciting. We then plod down to Loch Lyon through grassy hollows of the hills. We must be getting tired of the rucksacks; sensible people would take them up the Monk for a short descent E then NE into Gleann Meran. It's been a long day and the stone track along the loch batters my feet after all the hours of gentle squelching. Loch Lyon has tremendous surroundings but it is spoilt by the rubble along its edge. Still three miles short of our official day's end we camp above the loch, which is a reservoir, really. There's a dangerous cornice made of grass and I fall through it while fetching the water.

Foul Weather Alternative: Follow the West Highland Way south to Auch Gleann, then by the riverside track. Continue along the north side of Loch Lyon, where there's more track than on the map. An unusual five-Corbett day is available immediately south of Auch Gleann.

DAY 5
Loch Lyon to Killin
Stuchd an Lochain, Meall Ghaordie (or Ghaordaidh)
16 miles, 4900 feet 8½ hours

The Deity who presides over Feet and Legs says this: "After a day when you go well comes a day when you don't." This one has a cold start. The nice man on breakfast TV had said "Interestingly cold." We too are interestingly cold after overdoing it a bit yesterday. A cold start is a slow start. Our campcraft is sluggish with numb fingers and we need some WD40 on our spark plugs. Two hours to get away and there's those three extra miles on the start of the day to be made up to reach Killin before the shops shut.

Stuchd an Lochain is one of those less thrilling Munros. One of the advantages of Munro-bagging is that it gets you into these out-of-the-way places where no one ever goes because it's not worth going there to do it. We climb it by the track from Pubil and then over Meall an Odhar to take advantage of what ridge there is. The wide views from the top are the same wide views as yesterday. Then it's back to Pubil for the sacks.

A big ridge separates us from Killin to the south-east; we cross the bridge at Dalchiorlich towards Meall Ghaordie. Meall Ghaordie is better. Extensive foot repair and a large lunch at a pretty, crag-hung stream on the way up make the difference. It's not the scenery but the calories that lift the spirit. The descent from Meall Ghaordie is a good one on a small mossy path - a distinct advantage of an untrampled hill. This one teases its way down through grey flaky rock, black peat and heather to reach the shielings in grid square 5337. The map gets top marks for suggesting the strange terraced path along and above Glen Lochay. It's lovingly graded; its footbridges are

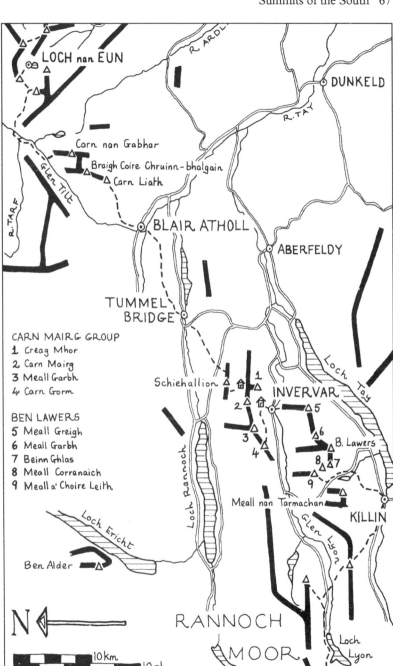

LOCH nan EUN

R. ARDLE

DUNKELD

R. TAY

Carn nan Gabhar

Glen Tilt

R. TARF

Braigh Coire Chruinn-bhalgain

Carn Liath

BLAIR ATHOLL

ABERFELDY

TUMMEL
BRIDGE

CARN MAIRG GROUP
1 Creag Mhor
2 Carn Mairg
3 Meall Garbh
4 Carn Gorm

BEN LAWERS
5 Meall Greigh
6 Meall Garbh
7 Beinn Ghlas
8 Meall Corranaich
9 Meall a' Choire Leith

Schiehallion

INVERVAR

Loch Tay

1

2

5

3

6

4

B. Lawers

8

7

9

Loch Rannoch

Meall nan Tarmachan

Glen Lyon

KILLIN

Loch Ericht

Ben Alder

N

RANNOCH

MOOR

Loch
Lyon

10km

10mL

fine ones with stone piers; chunks of wood, like railway sleepers, lie across the wet bits. They are railway sleepers. It is not a path at all but a forgotten narrow-gauge line. from 546354 there is a sudden plunge through woods of larch and birch beside a huge hydro pipe, green and riveted. Three miles of road make the feet feel a bit trodden in. We pass a man dropping poisoned worms into molehills. He doesn't get one of our cheery greetings. And so to Killin.

What a dump! Everything snaps shut at five except the Youth Hostel, which doesn't open until then. No moleskin - no chemist - and the shop, with just the socks I need, closed at four and doesn't open again until ten tomorrow. I find some socks that may help at the bottom of the rucksack. The Youth Hostel is crumbling into old age. Our truly gross meal of Scottish lamb, sausages, potatoes, salad, fried bread with marmalade and courgettes provençale attracts some comment from the fellow hostellers as they open their freeze-dried chille.

Control, friendly as ever, (Control's name is Barbara) say showers tomorrow, fine the day after. David is keen to do Meall nan Tarmachan as well as the six in the Lawers group tomorrow. I am less enthusiastic.

Foul Weather Alternative: Track southwards from Pubil (GR 459418) to Kenknock in Glen Lochay with Corbett, Meall nan Subh (GR 461398) if desired. Then road, I'm afraid, unless you want the two very dull Munros to the south. This is our worst FWA - even the track is tarred.

DAY 6
Killin to Invervar
Ben Lawers Group (6 summits)
19½ miles, 7900 feet; 11½ hours

The "Youth" Hostel is full of elderly dodderers (this includes us) complaining about rowdy behaviour of the Ultimate Challengers in Kingussie in 1978. Certainly Killin Youth Hostel could do with some rowdy behaviour. We are the only challengers to use the place this year; our route is commendably odd.

A good and greasy breakfast and we're off at 8.30 - good for a YH start. The sympathetic Warden has given us light tasks before our heavy day. The last two loaves in Killin are in our rucksacks, reinterpreted as marmalade sandwiches. The day is cloudy with only a little rain. We decide that 8000 feet of climb is enough fun for anyone and omit Meall nan Tarmachan from our plans. Gaelic speakers wonder at illogical English who pretend that the tarmachan is a Greek bird and spell it as Ptarmigan.....The Tarmachan and Lawers hang over Killin in wonderful knobs and look as if they are about to drop onto the main street. (Not a bad idea, really.) David decides that the Tarmachan is to be Baby Rosie's first Munro. She is to do one at one, two at two and so on. I am sure she'll enjoy it.

Slavish adherence to the map leads to a dull life so we attempt to repeat our fortuitous pathway trick from Ben Cruachan. This time it works less well and we fight our way through energetic trees. David closes the campaign with an epic battle with a fence, which the fence jolly nearly wins. An extra half-mile of A827 would have got us to the bottom of more heroic pipework at 584347. We reach the heroic pipework at last and climb beside it until it vanishes like a dragon into the hill and then walk the highest road pass in Britain (probably).

The route up Lawers from the Visitor Centre is an eroded track under perpetual repair. The stiles count you as you go over and every pathside rock has its ring of fag-ends. Respect the environment; choose another route.

As peak-baggers, ours is to walk north past the Lochan na Lairige to the cairn at the top of the road. A small path wanders off into Gleann Da-Eig. The cloud rises slowly up the side of Meall a' Choire Leith and so do we. As we poke our heads over the rounded ridge we find no rain but rather a lot of wind. The yellow grasses throb and thrum in the gale. Progress forward is a kind of demented dance as the wind tries to twist our rucksacks off. Twenty children are sliding down a small snowfield - it looks like Glenshee ski slopes. "We're too old for that," says David, regretfully, as we scamper over two more Munros (Meall Corranaich and Beinn Ghlas).

The top end of the path up Ben Lawers from the Visitor Centre resembles the Ordinary Route on the Eiger: that is to say a frightful heap of rubble where the main danger is that someone will kick a stone down on your head. We balance up to Lawers summit with wide-apart legs like drunken sailors. I cling to the cairn to be photographed. Between clouds that whizz past like 125 trains (but there's no yellow line to stand back behind) we glimpse the Lomonds of Fife and the distant eastern sea.

Over the summits east of the main one we are out of range of the Visitor Centre and heading happily into visitor periphery. An Stuc ("the sticky-up bit") has one of those steep descents where you look down and see only rocks and dwarf azalea and many little bits of path. "Not really steep," says David. The last one is Meall Greigh. With the wind behind, you could jump into Loch Tay three thousand feet below. David almost does so in pursuit of his woolly hat, which he brings down with a flying tackle - victory over the woolly hat.

We descend back into Glen Lyon, fifteen miles down the Glen from where we slept by the loch two days before. This is Scotland's longest glen and has a haunted castle halfway down, which the detour to Killin has helped us avoid. Most frightfully, the top half of the ghost haunts the bedroom and the bottom half, the graveyard. All four halves of us drop into the glen via a zigzag stalkers' path east of Creag Dubh. The zigzags are necessary; we could toss our rucksacks down the chimneys of the farmhouse below.

Invervar has one of the Scenic Phoneboxes of Scotland, set among larch and birch, red against fresh green. We have only one ten-pee so we leave a message for Barbara and wonder if any of the challengers were on Ben Nevis today - they would have been challenged indeed. Seen from Ben Lawers, Nevis sticks up into the wind like a bear hiding in a strawberry-patch.

There is also at Invervar an interesting Lint Mill, neatly built with wooden floors in a wooden situation beside a gorge. We reluctantly decide not to use it an informal bothy and go up a rhododendron track through mossy larches - an excellent start to the day but not quite so good after 7000 feet. David has decided that we are to go for a real bothy 1000ft above: he doesn't trust this weather (forecast, we recall, fine). So up we go. They must be popular these Mairgs though the only virtue seen from here across the glen is that they look easy for there are lots of noticeboards. INTERESTING LINT MILL. KEEP OFF DEER STALKING 15TH OCTOBER TO 14TH MAY ALSO 15TH MAY TO 14TH OCTOBER. NO CANOES, CAMPING. SSSI GO BY THE WEST. WEAR YOUR CRAMPONS. PATH EROSION EVEN A SMALL PET CAN FRIGHTEN A DEER. It must be remote here for they haven't got around to banning mountain bikes.

More zigzags, calculated with a methodical cruelty that is more Swiss than Scots: the path to your Alpine hut is uniformly just-bearably-steep for thousands and thousands of - not feet but - metres. Seventy-five deer run out of the corrie in the dusk. David doesn't see them for his eyes are fixed on the BOTHY. It is truly a goodie. Wood lined, wood benches and a table! It's in a sheltered slot of the hills with a little chuckling stream (followers: the Allt Coire a' Chearcaill and we're at GR 674497), splendid hills behind and a lovely view out through the notch where we came in. David is pleased with his discovery. We eat the bothy's tinned frankfurters even though it means carrying the empty tin for two days to Blair Atholl. We are still a day ahead and now, thanks to Beinn Mhanach, only two hills behind. We can pick them up in the East, where there are plenty of hills. Twenty climbed, twenty-one to go. Tomorrow is an easy day and soft on the feet.

Foul Weather Alternative: North-west then north through Lairig Breislich then north-east through Gleann Da-Eig to Invervar with optional Corbetts Beinn nan Oighreag, Meall nam Maigheach. Or for those tired of hills, why not visit the Visitor Centre?

DAY 7
Invervar to Glenmore Bothy
Mairg Group
11 miles, 3400 feet; 6 hours

Our bothy has unusually polite graffiti thanking the landowner. Some geologists were here in 1982 following the Erskine Schist. We hope they've caught it by now. We have an easy day over the four Munros of the Carn Mairg group, which are in cloud most of the way. Fine mountains these are if you're fresh in from England. After Ben Cruachan though, they really are a bit tame. From the bothy, traverse westwards till you can ascend the E ridge of Carn Gorm, then follow the stony ridge round over Meall Garbh. Carn Mairg may have been my hundredth Munro and Craig Mhor (unnamed 981m) was the expedition's twenty-fifth.

The mist rises to spare us some amusing navigation through the col west of Meall nan Eun. David is having trouble with his dodgy knee where the German skier hit it twenty years ago; he is bearing up bravely or perhaps not suffering much - it's hard to tell. Glenmore Bothy (GR 712527) is tricky to spot from above. We are within forty yards when we see a chimney-pot above a bank of heather. We were heading straight for it of course.

We arrive absurdly early at two-thirty. It's another wood-lined bothy looking at Schiehallion at point-blank range. Unfortunately Schiehallion isn't looking back for cloud sits down to two thousand feet. With fuel for the fire (we haven't any) we could have a really jolly afternoon drying our socks. Instead we go looking for the cave, Uamh Tom a Mhor-fhir. The name is long enough to cover a whole patch of country and we do not find the cave. But there's a neat little gorge you can travel down with a foot on each side.

It's still absurdly early. David reads Lord Jim. I haven't got a book so must write some limericks. The cloud remains at two thousand feet. Shall we get a view of Schiehallion tomorrow and will it be a view from sea to shining sea? Whilst running the Fort William Marathon (same day as the London Marathon and a lot easier to get into) I thought I saw Schiehallion from the shore of Loch Eil, which is the sea; but you think a lot of funny things whilst running the marathon.

Foul Weather Alternative: Brave the storm for a high crossing between Meall Garbh and Carn gorm for Glen Sassum (bothy) or Kinloch Rannoch. Today's optional Corbett Beinn Dearg, way out East.

DAY 8
Glenmore Bothy to Blair Atholl
18½ mile, 3200 ft; 9 hours.

The main thing today is to catch the shops at Blair Atholl. Six-fifty is a good start. The cloud on Schiehallion has shifted not a foot in the sixteen hours since we arrived; it might as well be glued on.

David has a bizarre urge to climb Schiehallion by its steep sides instead of the gentle ends. Fortunately, Schiehallion is on two different sheets of the map so I leave him with Sheet 52 while I take Sheet 51 up the sensible way. All relationships are improved by periods of separation.

Imagining the view, and David struggling over the boulders, up I go. The rock under my feet changes to quartzite. "The quartzite cap may in some lights be taken for snow." The light in question must be darkness: and there are many other facts about Schiehallion that are far more interesting. Because of its symmetrical shape and convenience to the tea-rooms of Pitlochry, Schiehallion was used as a balance weight with which to weigh the Earth. A plumb-line is deflected from the vertical by Schiehallion; Schiehallion being of known mass, the weight of the World follows. (How do you determine the vertical if not by a plumb-line? By taking sightings of the stars of course.) Let no one say that pure Science is useless; the mass of Schiehallion was not, in fact, known and they had to invent, in order to determine it, the contour line. Well, I think that is interesting.

As those who climb the Grey Corries already know, quartzite makes nasty scree and nice shattered ridges. I find one of the latter up in the mist. I decide that a snowball on the cairn will be an environmentally friendly way of telling poor David, still struggling in nasty scree, that I am in front of him; but the cairn already has two squares of chocolate on it. David is in front of me.

No view, but then it's not the view we go up there for - it's the fatigue poisons. A view is a useful distraction, it's true, for the slow bits before the endorphins start to flow; but some tricky map-and-compass-work does just as well. I destroy a cairn on the Tourist Path: there are so many cairns that they obstruct navigation. The Tourist Path is another scar but it's fun to run down the exposed peat and off the mountain at nine-thirty, before anyone else is on it.

Now comes the rough moorland where David, somewhere on the left, crept up on deer. He was gratified to see that even deer have trouble rushing around in this deep heather. I come down off Craig Kynachan through silvery-grey and fresh green birchwoods. Here the quartzite rocks are coloured birch-bark and the bilberry below is coloured fresh birch-leaf. This brightness is refreshing after high altitude colours with expressive Gaelic names such as glas (dark grey), ruadh (reddish brown), dearg (reddish black) and odhar (dappled ochre brown). I loop round the bend of a broad aqueduct and past a fine hydroelectric power station of Georgian style. All this, the reservoirs, the pipes through the hillsides and the hole under Cruachan is part of a massive 1930's engineering structure to make electricity in lots of middle-sized bits all over the southern Highlands. It works, it's cheap and, apart from the reservoir edges, does have a certain presence and style: in the same way one gets fond of the concrete trig points on hilltops.

A finer engineering work altogether is General Wade's stone bridge at Tummel. David is on the other side finishing off a meat pie. He was going to save half for me but decided not to. After some more intensive eating we go up through a long, hot forestry track for the one horizontal section that interrupts our hill-walk. The reason for the heat is not an uncommon one: we are being shone on by the Sun. As soon as we came off Schiehallion the cloud did too and disappeared into a fierce blue sky. We pass a mysterious shaft thirty metres wide and about a hundred metres deep with water at the bottom.

On the track, footprints all point east and are those of the Ultimately Challenged. After a few miles we meet two, who are carrying 40lb each along a wiggly low-level route from Lochailort.

High-level walking is easy. It's cities and forests I get lost in. Here the map sets a trap: at 846619 the forest road goes south-east (marked as a path). Take the lesser track (marked as the only one). It's a lovely needle-floored arbour that leaves the forest near Edintian and becomes a path through sunny fields that loses and then finds itself as it passes Tomanraid.

I begin to realize that there may be more to this low-level lark than the boring old forest tracks. The map tells you what the mountain is going to be like but you never know when you are going to find places like this green valley; now an avenue through parched rhododendron; then a purplish black moor with a single pine. We go over the curve of heather-clad mountains and a tiny, cairned path which drops and steepens, showing us Blair Castle, gleaming white across the valley. The path plunges through another wood of vertical

Schiehallion: with its views over half of Scotland a deservedly popular top. On Summits of the South you climb its unfrequented southern slopes. Reach the cairn before 8.00 am for assured solitude and clear, early-morning air.   *Photo: Jim Teesdale*

Spring birches, dashes across a wooden footbridge over the Garry and stops, slightly breathless, at the backs of the houses of Blair Atholl.

We find Gary's Mum's house. Gary's Mum is out being a guide at the castle but Frank gives us tea and shows us, more fascinating than any baronial interior, the washing machine. He asks us if the ethics allow us to sleep indoors. Yes indeed: our ethics are quite loose enough for that.

Frank entertains us with his tale of his shipwreck on Kerrera Island, off Oban. His boat crashed because while steering and dealing with a burst jib and being jiggled by a force nine gale, he couldn't lay his hands on three pipe cleaners to unblock the filters on his engine. He'd also lost his anchor in the previous emergency.

Gary's Mum says she gets puzzled by American visitors: one asked her for the "leaning armour". Answer tomorrow.

Foul Weather Alternative: West of Schiehallion by McGregor's Cave (GR 715586) and aqueduct.

DAY 9
Blair Atholl to Loch nan Eun
Beinn a' Ghlo (3 summits), Carn an Righ,
Beinn Iutharn Mhor
23 miles, 8500 feet: 11½ hours

The armour? It was tilting armour. There is serious news about Ian Botham. He has been put back in the team. I gather that Botham is extremely good at

Beinn a' Ghlo rises behind Blair Castle.

it but lacks the proper spirit. Surely anyone who walks across the Alps with an elephant (though the elephant got sore feet, didn't it) cannot be all bad?

We get away at eight, which for a start under a roof is good and a tribute to the understanding nature of our hosts. Cloud is just brushing the tops and we are aiming at a long day with a high camp.

David's map-reading leads us out on a beechwood path on the wild and rocky east bank of the Tilt. There's a grotto on the other side of the bank but the hermit is out. We climb the first thousand feet of the day up a tiny road, one-in-five all the way. It must be terrifying to come down in snow - even without a car - but, uphill, is more pleasing to our refined taste than a flat one would be. Pleasing at least to the unrefined feet gambolling about in their new socks: new socks, as the saying has it, new man.

Road then track leads east past Loch Moraig. The path up Carn Liath starts at 929682. It's a steep haul but steadily widening views give plenty of excuses to stop.

Beinn a Ghlo is a well-shaped mountain in silver and maroon. Broad, mossy ridges dip and swing among the three tops. Each of the three is a Munro.

The summits are getting easier to do if not to say, but here's a useful tip: use a casual English translation, it's easier to remember and gives the impression of fluency in the Gaelic without having to decide which one of the G's and H's is the crucial one which isn't silent. So the summits of Beinn a Ghlo become "Grey heap", "Small blisters" and "the Goat"- a crisp summary of the ultimate challenge experience though not as telling as the one we were to find in the picnic site loos at Glen Clova.

"If your nose is running and your feet are smelling then you're upside down."

Beinn a' Ghlo. From Carn Liath (Grey Heaps) looking towards Braigh Coire Chruinn-bhalgian (small blisters). These swooping high ridges give excellent walking. Beinn a' Ghlo escapes the general condemnation we extend to the Eastern Grampians.

The Lowlands are creeping up on us now. The Lomonds of Fife are lurking just beyond the second ridge until some kindly rain-clouds block them out and tuck us into our cosy world of ptarmigan, heather and heavy rucksacks. They're less kindly to David, who lacks waterproof trousers. David's damp legs prompt various route proposals.

We shall not tread the heather to Loch Loch - it's enough to know that such a place exists; one doesn't need to visit it. Instead we'll go the long way round by the top end of Glen Tilt to save time. We'll even divert to the bridge north west of Meall a Mhuirich to avoid getting carried away by the raging floodwaters of the Tilt. (This bridge at GR 956763 existed when I last crossed it in the summer of 93 and probably still does.)

David's third proposal is that we stop four hours early to find a sheltered camp. I want to try out my 2000 ft lochan. Besides, we might have to miss out on mountains to catch up so I say, "let's see what the weather does."

Glen Tilt is a long defile with the river still as wild and rocky as where we left it five hours earlier, and a long, wet wade if we hadn't gone for that bridge.

We meet the two forty-pounders of yesterday at Bedford Bridge (983796). This is a very bouncy suspension bridge over the Tarf waterfall where young Thomas Bedford drowned, wading. Rivers are an interesting feature of your low-level crossing, involving tests of nerve and sanity and the exposure of one's nakedness to the winds as an alternative to long unexpected journeys up boggy valleys. Up on the ridges you don't get much trouble with rivers.

Much of Glen Tilt is sad Landrover track but a quarter of a mile past Bedford Bridge we bear right and cross the now narrower river for a small over-the-moors path just north of Allt Feith Lair. This pretty little thing will gently lead us into realms of delight where the mountains rise into cloud, gorges plunge and stony slopes lead suddenly to a cluster of pink and green farmhouses (Fealar Lodge), where three white ponies dash away over the moor.

Alas the path, soured by much rejection, is hiding its sweet face among bogs and covering its open and trusting nature with a layer of heather-stalks and bog grass. There's a rebuke here to the unimaginative, who plough their furrow up and down Schiehallion and Ben Lawers. Ancient, unravished paths languish beneath the yielding heather of the East just waiting to be gently pressed by you in your big boots.

The rain has almost stopped and so we keep going. Beside a stony burn (034784), we find a green tent containing one of the Challenged. He has exactly eight days' beard and has not slept under a roof. His route has taken him all over the place but not in a straight line. That he is in this valley suggests that his ethics are sound. This is confirmed when he doesn't know how many Munros he's climbed.

We are unregenerate; the path has wound us up into a high pass and we dump our sacks and climb Carn an Righ. This "King's Heap" is an ignoble piece of peak-bagging: thirty minutes up - ten down and a view of clouds from inside. We are rewarded with six-hundred feet of old snow to run down. Then over Mam nan Carn to Beinn Iutharn Mhor, the last one of the day

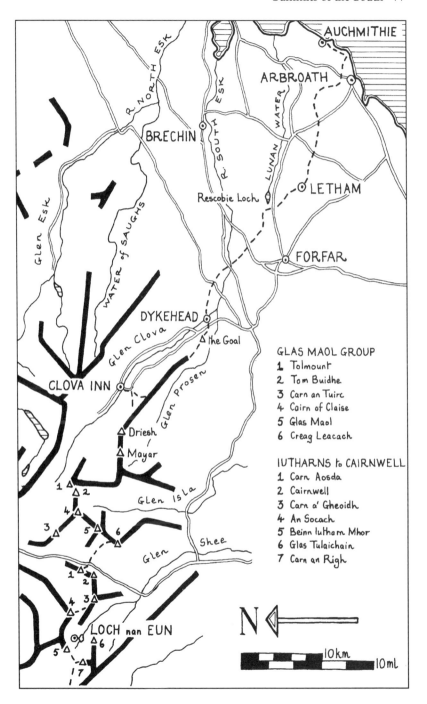

GLAS MAOL GROUP
1 Tolmount
2 Tom Buidhe
3 Carn an Tuirc
4 Cairn of Claise
5 Glas Maol
6 Creag Leacach

IUTHARNS to CAIRNWELL
1 Carn Aosda
2 Cairnwell
3 Carn a' Gheoidh
4 An Socach
5 Beinn Iutharn Mhor
6 Glas Tulaichain
7 Carn an Righ

N

10km
10ml

and the thirtieth of the trip. We are going rather strongly but this knocking off summits in the mist with the altimeter, watch and compass is simply flying on instruments without the aeroplane. My father navigates only to the nearest twenty degrees and says that this has made his days on the hills more interesting than they would otherwise have been.

Our campsite Loch nan Eun is well named. Eun is birds. There are two islands full of nesting gulls, the grass lush with oystercatcher guano. We pitch camp on a tiny peninsular with water on three sides. No burglar will surprise us coming into the tent but the loch might. It's a small loch though and a dry looking night with a pale blue wash of dusk across a wide sky.

We decide that, since the eggs have already been incubated, we shall not have any for breakfast. The birds on the islands are partying wildly all night and no amount of knocking on the walls of the tent will persuade them to shut up. However our long day with its mix of cross-country and up and down assures us a satisfying sleep at its end.

Foul Weather Alternative: East bank of Tilt to the Old Bridge (don't cross). Then up Glen Tilt to Bedford Bridge (GR 983796). Turn right as on main route by Fealar Lodge and through the pass Carn an Righ/Mam nan Carn. In dense weather a camp just short of this pass may be preferred.

DAY 10
Loch nan Eun to Glen Cova
Glas Tulaichean, An Socach, Carn a' Gheoidh,
Carn Aosda, Glas Maol Group (4 summits)
Tolmount, Tom Buidhe, Mayar, Driesh.
36 miles, 8500 feet: 15 hours

Followers with a head for figures may have spotted that those below the title for this day are rather large ones. Truly the original idea was to circle the Glas Maol Group clockwise, drop into Glen Isla and there stop: even this conception at 28 miles and 8000 feet isn't altogether moderate or sensible but, like all other addicts, Munro-baggers need an ever-increasing daily fix. My depraved appetite drives me out of the tent at five-thirty.

"Lovely day, shorts weather" - must apply David's First Law.

Just as the hills around still cling to the remnants of overnight mist, so David, at this early hour, still clings to some shreds of sanity. From inside the tent comes a mere incredulous grunt.

"Well it's not raining."

He finds this assertion more convincing. The sunrise is pale blue, flashing off our bird-infested loch. We're away at six-fifty up Glas Tulaichean - "Greenish-grey Hillocks" sound slightly dull but no hill is dull in the dark or at dawn. The moor between the hills is tough but we have views north to the snow-covered Cairngorms, where last year David camped alone on the Great Moss and liked it. To the south, the Lomonds of Fife are still sticking their little noses up. Ahead things roll lower and lower, already thinking of the North

Sea and the mudflats of Holland. We return to Loch nan Eun to pick up the tent, which has been drying in the early sun.

From Carn a' Gheoidh the hills are pleasantly tracked over the plateau and filling up with people as we approach the devastation of the ski area. What a mess we ski-ers make. Cairnwell is covered with buildings and Carn Aosda at 3007 feet, with tracks all over it, is the least worthwhile Munro yet, however easy to bag.

David has been contemplative for some time and now he empties the contents of his mind onto the grey pebbles. The early start, the good weather (only half a gale and practically no rain at all), the heady Munro-laden terrain mean that we can put a few miles and an odd wiggle into our day and do thirteen of the things. By now Munro-bagging is in the blood and to us even a small one, say Tom Buidhe, is more attractive than a warm campsite, a hot shower or indeed a rather large malt whisky. Our discussion therefore takes no account of the fact that valleys too can be pleasant places. One consideration dominates it: we can eat tomorrow's lunch right now.

We eat the two lunches at the Devil's Elbow road beside George and Maggie, who are fibreglass and gaze up at the surrounding hills from fibreglass sofas. George and Maggie are Art, part of the Sculpture Park - a clever scheme for who can tell, particularly with misted glasses, where sculpture ends and pylons for the Tee-bar begin? We make our way up the Blue Run and onto Glas Maol.

Glas Maol is two square miles of yellow grass and whistling air. Couples in jeans and macs give it a strange other-worldly atmosphere. David is grumbling. We are the only two inhabitants of Great Britain who don't know the result of yesterday's Cup Final. I stop a sporty looking young man and ask, while David, embarrassed, saunters on. I catch up and report: terrific match, neck and neck all the way - final score five-four to Motherwell. I have dared timidly to ask the English result as well and, by great effort, managed to hold all the no doubt fascinating detail in my head. Gazza sent off in the fifteenth minute and so on. Spurs had won and David says he supports Spurs so that's all right. Perhaps he will get over his disgust about Botham.

We gallop around the grassland, sometimes with the wind and sometimes against it. Eastwards at last into the evening and onto peat-hagged peaks Tolmount, Tom Buidhe - of no particular attraction except for the height. The going is tough over the moor southwards to Mayar. This over-indulgence is doing us no good at all. We're getting tired and arguing whether or not there will be any food at Glen Clova at ten. I am wrong; there will be food. There will be four filled rolls.

At eight-thirty the Driesh-Mayar ridge is the best for many hours - golden lit with plunging sides and a few jutting-out rocks. Driesh is our forty-third and last for we have run out of daylight and of hills together. The ones we've been on are all round us like friends crowding round to say goodbye. It's time to return to the valleys, where we belong.

We tumble steeply down over Hill of Strone into Glen Cova. Hill of Strone avoids tarmac, though the Winter Corrie in the dark is a truly fascinating challenge for those who are tired of life and want to end it. The bunkhouse at the Clova Inn is full but we can use the bothy, which is free to the Challenged and worth every penny. The bothy lies across a footbridge and has a working waterwheel. Some of the water from the working waterwheel comes in through the end of the bothy. We go for the balcony on the principle that filth tends downwards. The filth is nice and soft to lie on and the foam rubber most relaxing.

Original Intention: was to do the Glas Maol group from north to south, finishing over Creag Leachach and the Corbett, Monamenach for an overnight stay in Glen Isla. This makes a day long enough for all but the most degenerate Munro addict and takes in a pretty and seldom-visited glen. The final hill day could then ascend the Glencally Burn to Mayar and Driesh, thence south east along the ridge to Dykehead.

Foul Weather Alternative: Gleann Taitneach to Spittal of Glenshee (Hotel). Into Glen Isla by Loch and Glen Beanie.

DAY 11
Clova to the Coast
36 miles, 3000 feet, 13½hours

Today we decide to go for the coast, just for the sake of it and because I've never done more than 55 miles in two successive days. David has been going more and more strongly and is now almost unstoppable; he has agreed to go back up onto the fag-end of the Driesh-Mayar ridge to avoid the first ten miles of road. The original idea of this day was to do these two hills, which we greedily did yesterday, and follow their ridge as far into the lowlands as it'd go.

Back up on the ridge the view now is of lowlands, bright with yellow squares of rape seed and with distant flashes of the sea. There is tough heather tramping here; we are high but not high enough. After Cairn Leith there appears a useful shooters' Landrover track that leads us down to the last hill, which is called "the Goal". Here some of the gunmen are lurking in the heather with rifles. We wave cheerily and they give us dirty looks for we are making it hard for them to kill whatever they intend to kill today. At this time of the year it must be foxes, we suppose.

The track continues through fairly wild pine woods to the last slope of the Highlands, which is marked by a bizarre monument to Earl Airlie. It is a hundred feet high with a nondescript and weirdly pubic shrub around it. Earl Airlie died "as he would have wished" in battle - Diamond Hill 1902. Shot, presumably: there must be a moral in it for the grouse.

The Royal Jubilee Arms has been tastelessly renovated but its deep-fried lunch we find most tasteful. Now we are in different country: one where there are pubs and roads and the sun shines from time to time. The difficulty is not to travel on tarmac. Our first off-road excursion is blocked by elegant black gates: it's the Earl Airlie's back entrance. We took the farm track north of the river from Cortachy Home farm to Shielhill. Our second is interesting behind a sign "dangerous animals." We pass through herds of deer; two hundred of them range across a park in a Louis Quinze sort of way. This is the track by Auchleuchrie to Murthill. There is no assurance of any right of way along these tracks; I can only say that the farmer, when we met him, was perfectly friendly and reassured us that this time of the year we were not taking our lives into our hands. He said that the deer are interesting animals to handle.

You don't herd them but open the gate and wait for them to notice. Sometimes they get too tame and follow you into the house where they get their antlers stuck in the furniture.

My hope had been that various farm tracks and a disused railway would dodge most of the hard black tarmac sections but the farm tracks turn out to be private and the railway overgrown. In the end we tread roads like everybody else. We notice hippies in scruffy caravans. They grin and wave.

Various tracks, promised by the map, pass through raspberry fields, waist-high rape and a farmyard where David gets slightly nipped by a sheepdog. "It bit me," he says, incredulous and then, when I do not seem very surprised for sheepdogs are always nipping us hill-runners, "it BIT me!" He intimidates it with dreadful curses; I resolve never to bite David.

We taste the railway at Rescobie (from GR 485521) but it's too coarse even for our unrefined tastes and it's back to the road. The crossing of Dunnichen on an old grass road gives our first sight of Arbroath. The way ahead still looks very long - and very flat.

We're at Letham at six, still only half way across the plains. We stop for a drink at the Commercial Inn and refill the water-bottle. It's a friendly pub; nobody seems to think we're crazy. The hippies we passed were holding a festival on Dunnichen Hill to commemorate the first ever victory of the Scots over the English in AD 600. (Well you don't have to believe it if you don't want to.) We missed the festival by a half mile. Pity, we could have stopped for the night. It is suggested that in our smelly state we would have fitted in nicely but it's two whole miles back now. We wander into the evening, taking in a bar supper and a nature ramble along the railway into Arbroath (GR

619459 is the place to aim for). As the street-lamps come on we find the back-entrance to a campsite and stroll through caravan city looking for tent space. At ten-thirty we put up the tent and collapse inside. Just two miles to go.

Foul Weather Alternative: assuming you start like a sensible person at Glen Isla, a more sheltered route can be made by Glenmarkie Lodge, Corwharn (611m) and Glen Uig to Dykehead.

DAY 12
Arbroath to Auchmithie
2½ miles, 1 hour

At six in the morning comes a cheery greeting from another green tent. One of our fellow-Challenged had also rolled in at ten-thirty last night and pitched thirty yards away without either of us noticing. We are a bit pleased at having made the coast from Blair Atholl in three days but this man has done it in two - without the eighteen Munros of course.

From here a nature trail leads into Arbroath but we take the tracks through the potato fields and a wooded cleugh to Auchmithie. There are splendid views with a calm sea and warm biscuit-coloured cliffs - even the masonry of Auchmithie is warm biscuit. We take photos and paddle in the sea then walk back to the main road, where we shall once again become mere people on wheels, taking a bus to Montrose.

The Park Hotel at Montrose is a useful drying-out centre from which the Challenged can ease themselves back into the real world. It has lashings of hot coffee and people with stiff, deliberate movements. The indoor environment is still strange. We gather badges, certificates, tee-shirts and news of our fellow challengers. The man with the gone-to-sleep arm sensibly retired from the event. James, the solitary from Iutharns, arrives, his beard now eleven days old. He gets quite excited to hear there's a parcel for him here, but it turns out to be from himself: he'd decided that he did not need any clean clothes and sent them on ahead.

We have done forty-three Munros - the most ever is about fifty-six but that person camped in valleys and ran round them in clumps, which is not quite the thing. Les Dawes, the organizer, once did thirty-three so it's forgivable to do quite a few - isn't it?

Conclusions
It wasn't quite as difficult as I expected it to be. From Killin onwards we found ourselves very fit indeed and outstripped our schedule. It may be that on lower routes with their hard surfaces the effect of the improving heart and lungs is counteracted by the deteriorating feet and legs.

Staying high virtually all the time, we missed the chance of interesting and pretty valley ground but also the certainty of boring Landrover tracks and forestry. The final section through the Lowlands is hard work; we could have done it slower with more drinking.

DATAFILE
Our Schedule

Section Day/From/to	distance miles	ascent feet	time hrs	Munros number
1 Oban - Taynuilt	17½	1800	6¼	0
2 Taynuilt - Glen Kinglass	16	8200	10½	4
3 Glen Kinglass- Inveroran	16½	5000	9	3
4 Inveroran - Loch Lyon	21	8000	11½	5
5 Loch Lyon - Killin	16	4900	8½	2
6 Killin - Invervar	19½	7900	11½	6
7 Invervar - Glenmore Bothy	11	3400	6	4
8 Glenmore Bothy - Blair Atholl	18½	3200	9	1
9 Blair Atholl - Loch nan Eun	23½	8500	11½	5
10 Loch nan Eun - Glen Cova	36	8500	15	13
11 Glen Cova - Arbroath	36	3000	13½	0
12 Arbroath - Auchmithie	2½	0	1	0
TOTALS	234	62,000	113	43

Accommodation
Hotels:

Inveroran Hotel	Tyndrum 220/263
Clova Inn	015755 222

Youth Hostels:
Oban (62025), Killin (820456) and Glen Doll (Clova 236)

Bothies:

Glen Kinglass	Loch Dochard Stable GR 217418
Invervar	Nameless at GR 674497
Schiehallion	Glenmore
	Glen Sassum (GR 652541)
Blair Atholl	Glen Bruar, 5 miles north at GR 835737
Glen Clova	Jock's Road shelter, GR 233778

Shops:
Taynuilt, Killin, Blair Atholl, Letham. NOT Bridge of Orchy.

Tourist Information Centres:
OBAN   Argyll Square, Oban, Argyll PA34 4AN   Tel 01631 63122
PERTH Marshall Place, Perth, Perthshire PH2 8NU Tel 01738 38353
TYNDRUM Hotel,Tyndrum, Perthshire FK20 8RY Tel 018384 246)
KILLIN Main St, Killin, Perthshire Tel 01567 820254
PITLOCHRY 22 Atholl Road, Pitlochry, Perthshire PH16 5BX Tel 01796 472215
ARBROATH Market Place, Arbroath, Angus DD11 1HR Tel 01241 72609 /76680

Chapter Four

ROUGH GALLOWAY
Gatehouse to Girvan

Scotland in miniature: that's what the Tourist Board calls Galloway. Now Galloway has its own coast-to-coast route - Gatehouse to Girvan. It is only 49 miles but these 49 miles contain an intensity of experience missing from many longer trips.

The heart of the crossing is the twenty miles with 7500 foot of climb over the mountains between Talnotry campsite and the very minor road at Shalloch Pass. Here we go like an arrow (only slower) through the rough and heavy Galloways with never so much a path: the previous footprints in the bog are likely to be those of goats rather than humans. Here the last wild boar in Scotland was shot in 1973; here Robert the Bruce and his five hundred hill runners resisted the combined might of the English and Scots armies for fifteen years, after which their strength, suppleness and stamina were such that nothing could stand before them.

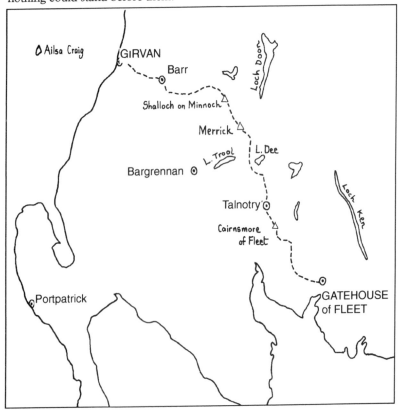

Can you run at 3 miles per hour?
An account of the Author's journey

Grey predawn sees us out of Gatehouse across a hummocky place covered in gorse bushes. The evening before I had tried to recce the place and run in a complete circle. Now we're navigating strictly by compass and expecting trouble. The gorse bushes try their best but we outwit them. Surprisingly, the path down the other side exists exactly as on the map. Perhaps it treads delicately round the knee-deep slurry at the bottom but we follow the compass straight through.

The Corse of Slakes road is an old military highway finding a new role in the modern world as a mud flume for tractors. Don't knock it; it's the only bit of real path on the whole trip! Meikle Bennan is an undulating heathery place leading to the old railway line. Under the the Clints of Dromore, a noticeboard welcomes us to the Cairnsmore Biosphere Reserve; Cairnsmore, it informs us cheerfully, is a high-rainfall granite bog of international importance.

I scramble up a rocky defile and bag two or three of the pretty little Clints. Glyn, despising the ignoble Clint-bagging, is hopping around in the forestry ditches below. The sun rises fast and so do we up the broad side of Cairnsmore (2200 ft). Behind us is a land and seascape with all the tonal splendours of the colour grey. In front is a nice flat bit leading along to the wide summit.

Beyond the summit Cairnsmore shows its true colours. The true colours of Cairnsmore are granite grey and peat black. They are presented first horizontally and then at an ever-steepening downward angle. Run down a granite slab, going faster and faster, then stop by dropping off the end into waist-high heather. Repeat the process until well shaken.

We cross the stepping-stones into the campsite just one minute behind schedule. "Not too bad," says Glyn. "After all that was a tough section." I phone Peter, who has just arrived at work and is going to slip away early to rendezvous at the next road-crossing in just eight hours' time. Meanwhile Glyn is being chatted to by the shop girl. The site's only been open three days and already she's starved of human company. "A party of Duke of Edinburgh girls equipped with a single gas burner and a rucksack full of microwave food....."

We tear ourselves away from the gruesome conclusion of her tale to scramble up the waterfalls and onto the woolly moors above. There are Christmas trees all round the edge but the middle has been left as Nature intended. All one can say of Nature's intentions is that Bannockburn must have been a doddle afterwards. We're ten minutes behind at Red Gairy Top. "Oh well," says Glyn, as he stops to pad his brand new running shoes with goat hair, "that was another tough bit."

"But Glyn, they cannot all be tough bits!"

But they are: twelve miles and six thousand feet, and the wild shores of Loch Enoch all silver and black between the hills, yellow with last year's grass. The Devil's Bowling Green is closed for the season and a little light

Typical Rough Galloway granite scenery around Loch Enoch.   Photo: Andy Priestman

sleet falls on our heads as we clamber up the Merrick. It's half past three and we're an hour behind. Merrick is only just half way and it's beginning to feel like a long night ahead. "I am going to check these measurements when I get home," Glyn mutters.

There are hill-walkers on Merrick: sensible ones who know that, in the month of April, one hill at a time is enough. Their cameras think they're indoors and try to illuminate distant Mullwarchar with flash.

"Which way did you come up then?"

"Oh we came up from Gatehouse. It's over there..." We hobble off before they can ask more embarrassing questions and try not to think of Peter slipping away early to meet us. If Peter knew knew he could go home, have his tea and watch the first half of Neighbours.

Now the unintelligent schedule is working on our behalf. The range of the Awful Hand, though wild, is also high. The Atlantic winds do what the goats cannot and keep the grass down. The viewing is still only in black and white but this does make the hills we've been over pale into the haze so that they look very far away indeed. Unfortunately it has the same effect on the hills in front. With fresh goat-hair in his shoes, Glyn gallops away strongly.

What Glyn hasn't realized is that there are two minor road crossings at the end of this stretch. It is necessary to fortify the spirit in advance for the 2.6 miles of heather bog between the two and Glyn has failed to do this. By the time we reach Peter at the Nick of the Balloch, Glyn's indomitableness has taken a severe dent, which even Peter's ambrosial rice cannot quite put back.

"Oof, oof." This is his way of saying, "Both ankles have gone and the old groin from the Bob Graham Round but don't think I'm going to stop." After all there are only sixteen miles and the sun's not down yet. Peter drives home to fetch some Girvan athletes out to Barr. With the promise of these kindly guides we agree to separate. I am to go for a sensible time, Glyn is to practise his night running for the Fellsman Hike.

There's something about 600 feet of steep short grass with not a path on and the sky peeping over the top - no use trying to explain it for it goes beyond logic. At the top is a grassy ridge, almost flat and shooting into the twilight. It's down with the throttle and hey! I head for the open road. A few undulations later it's a gate, then some tractor marks, then a sunken lane between two hedges: then a farmyard and the evening smoke rising above the pretty village of Barr. I've done 6.5 miles and 1200 feet in 90 minutes and crossed into Ayrshire: not bad for an old dog that's had quite a day already.

There's no let up at Barr. The pacers that Peter has kindly provided have combined ages which about match my own. Did we really climb 700 feet in 19 minutes? There's some disagreement about this as it's getting too dark to see the watches. Colin leads with assurance but this is Tom's first experience of hill-running and he's surprised to learn that hill-runners do not actually run up hills. Soon he'll discover we don't always run down them either.

Disdaining the torch, Colin takes us through the tussocks and bogs, helpfully indicating the streams by falling into them. "Troweir Hill," he says. "Saugh Hill. Doune Hill." Suddenly the ground drops away and we are looking at the lights of Girvan, 700 feet below.

Now this is something I'm usually rather good at.

Well, Colin's rather good at it too.... but I do draw ahead of Tom by a couple of paces on this steepish descent. The street lights twinkle by. "2.3 miles to go," Colin jokes. "3.6," I reply. What laughs. Dark sea slaps on either side of the pier and the smell of salt water is overpowering; I expect I am salt-depleted. There's a green light at the end of the pier and a low wall painted white to stop against and gaze out over the invisible sea towards the invisible islands. Colin produces a pair of trousers from somewhere and puts them on.

I am already asleep on Peter's floor when Glyn rolls in an hour later. "Excellent run," he says. "Excellent. But I'm going to have a look at those measurements."

So you think you can run at 3 mph? If you can there's a sort of record there for the taking. 49 miles; 15000 feet and it's 17 hr. 23 min. 37 sec. Don't leave it too long; the heather gets deeper every year.

Route Guide

From the bridge that spans the River Fleet in the centre of Gatehouse, head out of town on the westbound Newton Stewart road. At the end of town, where the road bends left, take the residential cul-de-sac to the right. It bends uphill. At a wooden bench take the right-hand fork. After 300 yards go through a metal gate on the left, marked "Public Footpath". Follow the path between houses onto the hill, where its waymarks are lost in tall gorse. A compass bearing of 278° leads over the crest, where a muddy track beyond a gateway leads down through the forest. Turn right on the road at the bottom and immediately left on a sunken cart track, which is the Corse of Slakes

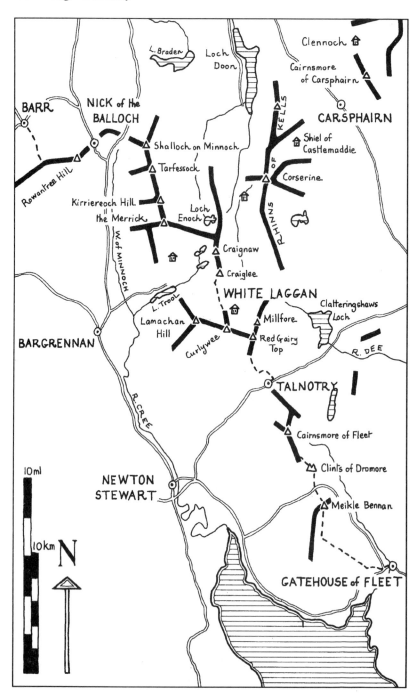

Road, (marked Old Military Road on the map hereabouts). Climb this for three miles to the tarmac road (GR 548582).

Take the Arkland farm track until it bends right away from the Skyre Burn, then field edges onto open hill. Climb Stey Fell, then Meikle Bennan. Descend north of Bennan to meet the B796 where it enters the trees, and follow it for two hundred yards to a tee junction. Take neither arm of the road but go ahead through a large wooden gate on a forest road and immediately right on the course of an old railway. On your right are the remains of Gatehouse Station. Here is the place where Richard Hannay alighted in 'The Thirty-nine Steps'.

Follow the railway under a bridge to the end of the forest, where a gate on the left and a noticeboard mark the start of a faint uphill path to a gap in the low but impressive Clints of Dromore. Go up on grass and granite for thirty feet. A rocky gully on your right with a goat path (and probable goat) leads to the top. Turn left and follow the Clints westward.

The shortest way now is to bash down right, through heather bog, to the top of the trees behind the Clints. Wheelmarks highlight the passage due west onto the steep flank above the Door of Cairnsmore. Here a fence can be followed straight uphill.

N.B. A drier way will be found over the pleasant hillocks of Craig and Culcronchie, giving fine views of Cairnsmore's craggy end. Eye this but do not try it; the granite lumps of the Door of Cairnsmore are rounded and sodden and provide fun of the most alarming sort, especially in descent. Instead cross the wide col and traverse right below the rocks on a sheep path. Soon you can climb to join the fence already mentioned. Coming the other way, the ridge descending from the Knee of Cairnsmore takes particular delight in dumping you at the top of these cliffs and it is essential to swing east along the fence.

An easy and pleasant grassy plateau rushes you forward over the Knee of Cairnsmore (the most southerly of the 'Donald' tops) to Cairnsmore itself. The summit is a bare, stony place with a huge cairn, a trig point and a memorial to pilots. Many planes have come to grief here on Scotland's final hump. Sea gleams around half the horizon, but you're likely to be looking northward where rather a lot of hills have now appeared.

Continue over Meikle Mulltaggart, and the nameless lump one kilometre to the north, to delay your descent onto (or into) the granite bogs around Coo Lochans. Flat granite slabs provide some relief as you climb Craignelder.

The ridge off Craignelder bears north-westwards then 346°, defined mainly by steep ground to the left. The small path goes invisible where it crosses bare granite, which is often. Aim for the forest ride at GR 493711(The forest extends further uphill to the west of the ride.) The bearing from the crucial point to Murray's Monument is 334° magnetic. A broken stone wall will be found in the ride and a rough path, that leads to stepping stones and the Talnotry camp site.

Head through the site to its northern corner, where a break in the wall lets you out onto the verge of the A712. Pass the monument and cross the road bridge over the Grey Mare's Tail Burn. Turn left along the bank of the stream, noting the path heading up the hill to your right. Having admired

The Grey Mare's Tail at Talnotry.

the waterfall go directly up the slopes behind you on a tiny steep path to rejoin this more prominent path, which is way-marked as the Blue Trail. Stick with the Blue as it crosses a forest road and climbs the east bank of the Grey Mare's Tail Burn beside more falls. The trail crosses the burn on a foot-bridge (GR 489728). Path builders here have given up the strug-gle with the peat and peeled the whole lot away to leave you walking on bedrock. The trail climbs south-west; at its highest point a clear but wet ride leads through the remaining trees onto the open slopes due west of the summit of the Fell of Talnotry.

Climb the Fell of Talnotry and then over moorland that becomes less tough as you go up (but unfortunately you have to go down at first) over Drigmorn Hill and Red Gairy Top. Red Gairy is the unnamed one half a mile SW of Millfore.

Descend past the White and Black Lochs. Waterproof granite is the reason for these ridge-perching pools. The humpy ground is great for hide-and-seek, a game that these two stretches of water like to join in.... in mist I once walked right around the White Lochan. The contours are confusing but the compass will get you there in the end.

The Loup of Laggan (at 457761) is a perfect little pass. The abrupt crag-gy slope of Curleywee above looks like a mountain, although, at 2210 feet, it isn't really. The path through the Loup is well defined. When you locate it simply turn uphill to the pass.

From the Loup climb westwards beside a stone dyke onto the plateau for the steep haul to Curlywee's airy top. (This for the southbound traveller is the tricky one. Descend off Curlywee on 325° from 250 yards to the end of a narrow, flat-topped spur. Now change direction sharply to 204° and continue on this along the plateau below until you find the wall.)

Coming off White Hill take a bearing for the western extremities of Loch Dee, which is still out of sight. If you get too far west you will get onto rough ground where rock ribs are divided by runnels of upright bog. It's not dangerous - you cannot go tumbling down the hill when you're sunk in mud above your knees.

The track you cross at the foot of White Hill is the uninspiring Southern Upland Way route through the Galloways. To the west it gives an easy escape from these difficult hills. If you want the White Laggan Bothy you turn right and right again after a mile, on a mud path through trees.

Our route goes straight ahead. A hideous bit of Galloway shrubbery is avoided by crossing the valley bottom on the sandy beach at the foot of Loch Dee.

Continue over the rocky crest of Craiglee and skirt the Dow Loch (not to be confused with the Dow Loch on Craignaw just over a mile to the north.) Descend due north across the rough bouldery valley. The south-facing crags of Craignaw present no serious obstacle as several streams draining the plateau provide grassy entrances.

The plateau above should be the most frightful bog but the abundance of granite slabs makes it more like a city pavement. Craignaw, though not the highest, is the wildest of the Galloway Hills.

A wrong (western) ridge leads off Craignaw but allow it to think it's tricked you for five minutes, then traverse right to gain the ridge running NW below its awkward first drop. This should lead you into the little col at 457836. A sharp five-metre climb leads to a plateau running north-west. Here granite pavements, dotted with erratic boulders, are known as the Devil's Bowling Green. A small path is forming. It leads to the fine cairn in the Nick of the Dungeon (454844) before the next rise.

Clamber up three gentle granite steps before bearing left to Loch Enoch's SW corner; a small cairn marks the col between Lochs Enoch and Neldricken, where our route crosses 'Not the Southern Upland Way'. A squelchy path leads along Loch Enoch's southern shore through the widely-scattered remains of an aeroplane that landed in the loch during the Second World War. Over two hundred planes and even an airship have been lost in these hills.

We now aim for Merrick. A third of the way up its south-east flank you leave the granite, perhaps with sadness, for it is this rock that has given the central part of this walk its savage landscape. Then again perhaps it's with a little relief. Merrick is just half way to Girvan but now you have two-thirds of the climb and all the really rough ground behind you.

After the introspective hollows of the last six miles, the rocky slopes give widening views and an increasing sense of freedom. The Merrick is the highest peak between the Highlands and the Lakes. On a cold, clear day in Spring or Autumn, look carefully to the North. Ben Lomond and the Arrochar Alps can be seen from here with the U-shaped glacial trough that holds Loch

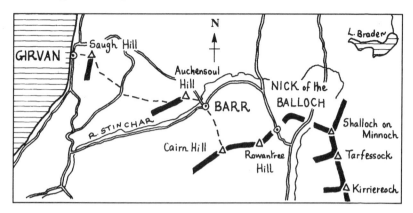

Lomond in between.

From the summit of Merrick head northwards on an attractive steep-sided ridge, the Spear of Merrick, and climb Kirriereoch Hill. The descent north of Kirriereoch is steep and rocky. It can be made less so by descending gently to the west for five minutes before turning right and plunging over the edge. Continue along the high grassy ridges to the trig point on Shalloch on Minnoch and descend the broad slopes to its north-west top (unnamed 659m.) As the ground gets lower it gets slower and the crossing of Shalloch (542m) to the minor road is cursed with peat haggs and unfriendly grasses. Cross the road and the Pilnyark Burn at the top of the plantation.

Go over, not round, Eldrick Hill - this is not mere peak-bagging but the easier way, avoiding much of the hostile herbage.

"We couldn't quite work out which hill they were pointing at," say the surveyors apologetically. "We couldn't follow their accent and besides, the midges were awful bad." So two of the hills you have just crossed were called Shalloch and the next one is the first of your Pinbecks. (Only two Pinbreacks? That's nothing; there are five Bennans.) Cross Pinbreack Number One or take the top of the forest to its south to reach the road at the Nick of the Balloch.

From the Nick of the Balloch, the diversion to Brandy Well is scarcely worth the effort; the alcohol content is very low. Ascend the steep short grass slopes to Rowantree Hill (552 m) and cross four small tops to Cairn Hill. The descent from Pinbreck Number Two is thigh-deep moss but the rest is rather restful. From the ancient cairn, descend past the sheep-handling area at Darley. Now a rough, but improving, tractor trail passes the puddle of Dinmurchie Loch and runs by the forest edge and then straight down to Barr. A footbridge leads out onto the main street of the attractive white-washed village.

Cross the river Stinchar on the B794. Turn right on the road and, in a few yards, a woodland path leads up onto Auchensoul Hill, which you climb. Descend on open grassland south of the main stream (westwards) to pass right of the building at Dupin, where a track is found. Follow the upper branch but stay below the quarry to the minor road at Tormitchell. Turn right along the road to the first buildings then left to cross the stream on a track. This track and its succeeding rough path could be followed through the gap of Laggan Loch and down to the roundabout at the south end of Girvan to finish along the urban foreshore. The more striking finale, however, is to leave the track as soon as it stops being usefully uphill. Go straight up the gentle ridge west, then north west to Troweir Hill. North from there, on the way to Saugh Hill, it is wet underfoot but the attention is distracted by the vastly greater quantities of water out to the West, broken only by the thousand-foot knob of Ailsa Craig. Ailsa Craig is the only island in the world to have two different vegetables named after it - an onion and a tomato.

The highest point of Saugh Hill is the tumulus, not the trig point. As you drop over the edge, Girvan finally appears below; a good strong leap will take you directly over the town into the sea. Failing that, slant down westward, crossing two streams to pick up a path and gate onto the Fauldribbon farm track. This leads to a street, which, if followed undeviatingly, leads to the end of the pier.

DATA FILE

Schedule for runners

Distance and Climb	miles	ascent	hours schedule	hours actual
Gatehouse to Talnotry	14.2	4600	4.28	4.33
rest			.20	.11
Talnotry to White Laggan	6.0	2700	2.12	2.45
White Laggan to Nick of Balloch	14.6	5400	5.02	6.17
rest			.20	.10
Nick of Balloch to Barr	6.5	1100	1.54	1.32
Barr to Girvan	7.8	1300	2.11	1.56
TOTAL	49	15000	16.26	17.20

Time
I append the above schedule for runners who want to do it in a day. Three or four days would be reasonable for a party of strong walkers. This is not a route for the unfit! To achieve a crossing without a tent you will have to accomplish White Laggan to Barr in a day, which is 22 miles and 6500 feet of ascent. Otherwise it would be necessary to divert from the route.

Terrain
The greater part of the route is pathless. There is pleasant high-level ridge-walking on Cairnsmore of Fleet and the range of the Awful Hand from Merrick to Shalloch. The last third of the walk is on grassy tops. However the central section of the walk is serious stuff - "worse than the Rhinogs", suggested the competitors on the 1986

Karrimor Mountain Marathon though this is putting it a bit strongly for nothing can be worse than the Rhinogs of Southern Snowdonia.

On the silver beaches of Loch Enoch you are as far away from civilization as you can be outside the Highlands. Combine this with the almost total lack of formal accommodation and you have a route whose noble austerity holds it quite above the common run.

Time of Year
There is not the same risk of seriously nasty weather here as in the Highlands so the walking season is longer. We went in April: sixteen hours of daylight, which should be enough. The undergrowth was ungrown and there was the amusing possibility of snow showers. At any time of year you would have to be very lucky to get accumulations of snow such as to require an ice-axe. May and June are as good here as anywhere. In July and August there will be midges, rainfall and crowded bothies; most of us do our long walks in these months. September and October can be good, for even bogland grasses change colour in interesting ways in Autumn. Short daylight is inconvenient. You should not plan to be walking in the dark but if the moon is waxing or full and the sky is clear the night can be the best part of the day.

Direction
This is a good walk (or run) either way. We went northward, hoping to see the sun set behind the Isle of Arran, but arrived three hours too late.

Equipment
If not a tent, then a bivvi bag is essential. If you have no experience of walking rough ground in trainers then this is no place to gain such experience.

Maps
O.S. Landranger 1:50000 Sheets 76, 77 and 83. Harvey's "Galloway Hills" at 1:40000 has useful extra detail of the serious central section between Talnotry and the Shalloch road-crossing but does not quite reach far enough to replace Sheet 77 altogether.

Access
No deer, no grouse. Cairnsmore is a Nature Reserve: respect this. Between Talnotry and Cairn Hill the Forestry Enterprise wants you to camp only at their two campsites. After long dry spells (which do occur from time to time) guard against forest fire, especially in late Spring before the new grass grows up through the old.

Transport
Gatehouse has several buses a day to Dumfries and Stranraer. For more information ring D & G bus information service on 0345 090510. Girvan has trains to Glasgow and Stranraer.

Chapter Five
THE SOUTHERN UPLAND WAY OR NOT ?
Experiences of the Official Route
And Suggestions for its Improvement

As I travelled across on the bus, the rain was coming down like a depressing totalitarian regime. The only sign of our path was one that said "This isn't the Southern Upland Way". Over in the East the setting sun shone pink on the vast surfaces of the nuclear power station. David was in the bar of the Co'path Hotel, smiling mysteriously into his beer. Of course, David's done this sort of thing before.

Messing around on the beach at Cove meant a slow start but then fifteen miles for the first day isn't too challenging - or is it? This idea of walking on and on for days...weeks... can the human frame take it at all? Will I hurl myself into a Southern Upland bog screaming "No no not another step"?

We stroll pleasantly among gorse bushes and cowpats and down through the trees to Abbey St Bathans. Exotic birdsong distracts me and I peer through the leaves. "It's a thrush," David says dismissively. My house in Sanquhar lies above the thousand foot contour - the curlew and peewit are fine noises but not music. Odd that most of this Upland Way is below the level of my home.

Loch Trool. A road west of the loch allows many walkers to avoid this, one of the really nice bits of the Southern Upland Way. Trool is a typical glacier-bottom loch where descending ice has gouged a hole in the flat valley floor. Geology begets landscape. Galloway, like Snowdonia, the Lake District and the Highlands, shows glaciated shapes: corries, trough-valleys and truncated spurs. The rest of the Southern Uplands have been washed into shape by rain.

I challenge David to think up a new joke about feet for the Sanquhar Pantomime, which is 'Cinderella'.

"Isn't that what you call a court shoe?"

"That's right Sir; it was the other one that got away".

David's job is to study and assist people who have injured their heads and lost part of their grammar and language. He asks them to recount Cinderella and they can never explain about Buttons. I cannot explain about Buttons either. He is like the Matterhorn, he's just there.

Longformacus has a hotel and a B & B but the hotel has become a conference centre for hard-line Christians and Mrs Amos is out. An extra 15 miles to Lauder would be one of those little unforeseen events that put the bubbles in life's vinegar but Mrs Amos has just gone up the road to see if she is expecting anyone tonight. We have tricked her by sneaking up from the wrong direction. Most walkers follow the book from west to east but David has already done Wainwright's one backwards and said we were to save the tough and interesting bits till last.

A good B & B, and Mrs. Amos is good, is a soothing experience. To be addressed as 'boys' in your thirty-seventh year; to be fed a whopping great cooked breakfast and sugar ricicles in those little packets my children squabble over; to be offered a nice cup of cocoa before going to bed, which has a pink candlewick cover and matching little heart shaped cushion (useless to any human sleeper but handy for your teddy)- such wholesome infantile regression usually comes at twenty guineas for a fifty minute session.

Day Two is a little dull apart from the first small slops of bog and a couple of cairns the size of beehives if bees were the size of poodles. The body is settling into the groove and beginning to enjoy the simplicity of one foot down and then the other.

"Sorry we're full up", says the warden at Melrose, "Edinburgh's your nearest, or Newcastle." This is a joke; the Youth Hostel, a wide Victorian villa with space for two dozen wide Victorian pedestrians with their booted wives, paintboxes, stout ash plants and all, will sleep tonight just six. The room with the view of the floodlit abbey has been frosted over and plumbed up for showers but we enjoy the high ceilings, the wide stairways and the feeling of endless empty space all around. Perhaps the place could be sold; the proceeds could maintain a small fleet of limousines to carry all those who wished between Portpatrick and Cockburnspath, together with a vanload of Youth Hostel mushy peas, mince from tins and powdered soup. We eschew denatured Youth Hostel food and find a good chippie.

David doesn't want to climb the Eildons. Perhaps he's heard about Thomas the Rhymer, who fell asleep there and was kidnapped for seven years to entertain the Queen of the Fairies. David, your shoe jokes were not that good....

Interesting industrial landscapes of old prams and the back of the Galashiels Sewage Works are followed by the nice grassy Minchmoor with more beehive cairns. We are staying with friends in Traquair, a good plan if you can; one is so jolly and sociable after eighteen miles on the road.

But 33 miles on Day Four is really.....rather ....a ....l o n g.....w a y. Perhaps the lunchtime beer at Tibbie Shiels was not such a good idea - perhaps the fifteen years of smoking cigarettes were not such a good idea - perhaps the 33 miles.

The nine miles of road is definitely a trudge (we'd intended to do the ridge to the North but not if we were to get to Beattock). After Ettrick Pen exhaustion was setting in, the faces turning white and the conversation running dry as the rain ran wet. And oh, the B & B's are all at the other end of town. We got the last bar supper in Beattock before they locked up the ovens and threw the scraps to the pigs.

I may have given the impression that there wasn't anyone else on this Way. That is quite incorrect. We met two by St. Mary's Loch and, on the fifth day, we met another - a real backpacker with tent and stove and all. We tried on his rucksack and staggered a few steps. The thing was just about possible, we supposed but why should one want to forgo the infantile pleasures of the B&B? At that time I hadn't discovered that in a small tent with rain on the roof you regress right back to the womb.

I would never suggest that you use the fabric of our historical heritage as a climbing crag but there's a nice little route at Cambridge called the Bridge of Sighs. The interesting bit is at the start where you edge round a buttress, facing outwards, with the dark and smelly river waiting for your body below. Then you have to fall sideways, a move that once done cannot be undone, and you get your hands on the large holds of the bridge proper. Now cling to the bars that serve instead of window glass and wait for a wandering scholar to cross the inside of the bridge for a refill of midnight oil. Just as he passes, greet him out of the night sky. Now you know what it feels like to be the invisible man.

In the same way I passed along the pavement of my home town in big boots and a dirty old shirt - invisible. I said "Hello Robert", softly as he past us. He jumped on hearing my voice out of the empty air.

David in his shorts has a more corporeal presence. "Braw legs!", they had cried at the bus stop as he passed by.

He needed the encouragement. That 33 mile day had changed everything. Now we were drawing up energy from reserves and spending it before ever it could jingle in our pockets. But then, after two days when 15 miles seemed like a long one, we broke through a new energy level - bouncing fit and eating miles like currant buns.

The SU Way through the Galloways hides among the trees to avoid having to look at those horrid hills. It won't do, it won't do at all. We abandoned it and bounded over Curlywee and Lamachan, where there's a bit of a ridge with rocks.

The path along the Loch and then the Water of Trool is one of the good bits, especially in the evening when the sun casts tree shadows across the lilies. The fatigue of fifteen years of cigarette smoking had finally been blown out of our lungs but a new addiction had seized us. Two hundred and ten miles are not enough. How about our own route across the proper Scotland - across the Highlands? That is for next year but more immediate cravings must be satisfied - let's use the fitness now for a day-tour of the Lakeland Three-thousanders.

Bits of sea appear on all sides. The Lake District is back over our left shoulders, Ireland appears ahead. I want to reach Portpatrick by noon for a 9 1/2 day crossing but the final cliff path is so tasty we slow and savour it.

And that's it. No sign or monument marks the western end of the way. You simply wander along the harbour, gradually ceasing to be a long distance walker and becoming another person looking for an ice cream, a copy of the Guardian and a bus stop.

Distance & Climb

Stage		distance miles	climb (ft) E - W	W-E
1	Portpatrick - Castle Kennedy	13 ½	700	600
2	Castle Kennedy to New Luch	9 ½	500	400
3	New Luce - Bargrennan	17½	1200	1200
4	Bargrennan - Dalry	24	1700	1700
5	Dalry - Sanquhar	27	3200	2900
6	Sanquhar - Wanlockhead	8	2000	900
7	Wanlockhead - Beattock	20	2900	4200
8	Beattock - St. Mary's Loch	21	3000	2500
9	St. Mary's Loch - Traquair	12	1300	1600
10	Traquair - Yair Bridge	9 ½	1700	1900
11	Yair Bridge - Melrose	7 ½	700	700
12	Melrose - Lauder	9 ½	1000	800
13	Lauder - Longformacus	15	1600	1400
14	Longformacus - Abbey St Bathans	7 ½	800	1000
15	Abbey St Bathans to Cockburnspath	10	800	1100
	Totals	212	23000	22900

Guides to the Southern Upland Way

We used the guide by Ken Andrew only till lunchtime on the first day. The waymarking on the route is first rate: even the map stayed in the rucksack most of the time. ALL guidebooks are west to east.

O.S. 1:50000 Landranger maps covering the route are numbers 82, 76, 77, 78, 79, 73 and 67.

The Southern Upland Way: The Official Guide Roger Smith (HMSO 1994) - Full of interesting information and colour photos, none of which you actually need. The maps are long thin diagonal strips of Landranger. It costs twice as much as any other guide (probably because of the photos) but half as much as buying all the separate Landrangers.

Southern Upland Way: The Official Guide by Ken Andrew (HMSO 1984) 2 volumes. Much cheaper than Roger Smith's. The same useful Landranger strips but in the out-of-date First Series version - still good enough, given the waymarks.

Along the Southern Upland Way by Jimmy Macgregor (BBC) - Anechdote and photos - a good way to get the flavour but no maps or route description.

A Guide to the Southern Upland Way by D. Williams (Constable) - It is hard to go astray with the Southern upland Way: the only lost person I met was using this guide. The maps are really out of date being the old Bartholemew's at half an inch to the mile. If you enjoy the thrill of exploring the unknown this one is for you.

Accommodation Leaflet
Useful but not usually up to date. Available from the Tourist Information Centre, Whitesands, Dumfries. Tel 0387 53862

GOING OFF THE SOUTHERN UPLAND WAY

"Once I had descended to Yair Bridge from the Three Brethren I had little more to look Forwards to"
Mike Cudahy from *Far Trails to Wild Horizons*

"The first sixty miles to Dalry are the worst, quite unrecommend-able.... I didn't know the Lammermuirs and, after plodding through them in thick mist on a bulldozed road, I still don't. The bar at Longformacus has closed"
Steve Clarke: *Strider* Magazine 1992

We say of 1930's furniture: superb workmanship, frightful design - and far too much timber. It's the same with this path. The line across the country is good, the maintenance and waymarking are first class, but it's so easy when a problem of access comes up to say "oh we'll send them round by the road."
The trouble is that Scotland doesn't have a network of red dashes on the map indicating rights of way; inspiration, luck, legend and local knowledge have to serve. The other trouble is that, from the onset, the Forestry Commission said "Do put your path through any of our bits". They have rather a lot of bits in Southern Scotland.
A few of us, however, have managed to enjoy this path. If you do not like boggy bits (they have all been built over), or if you don't like your fellow walkers, then this is the one for you. I particularly recommend it to three types of traveller:-

Novices
Runners
Those Not on the Southern Upland Way

Novices
The stages are short and so is the herbage underfoot. You are unlikely to get lost and if you do there's a road a few miles away. Walk fast, whether fast for you is two and a half or ten miles an hour, and walk light. Certainly you need not bother with a tent. A tent will ruin your walk, as it did for Steve Clarke (quoted above). Fifteen pounds is probably too much to carry: I would aim

for ten. The only long section, Sanquar to Dalry, is broken by a bothy, the only one in Scotland with a flush toilet. Send your sleeping bag in advance to Sanquar or Dalry. This is a very suitable route to experiment with novel long-distance techniques. Try the deliberate hilltop bivvy or change your boots for trainers.

Runners

This really can be the answer! Running gives you something to think about on those less interesting sections and it also gets you across them sooner. Mike Cudahy is, it's true, a runner; he simply cannot have been doing the dull bits fast enough.

The most recent record is Mike Hartley's in 1988. He took 55 hours 55 minutes, of which about three hours was standing still. That will have been a supported run. Doing it with a bivvi bag or between B & B's might take five days.

Runners who do not want to do it all can do it in bits. There is a SU Way Relay Challenge. The rules for this are:

* Teams of five or less.
* Run east to west.
* All runners must do the first and last legs.
* The remaining 208 miles may be divided among the runners in whatever order and with whatever changeover points they chose.
* Night runners must have a companion, who need not be a member of the team.
* Notify the head of Outdoor Education for the Dumfries and Galloway Region, who will authenticate your run.

The current record is 30 hours 10 minutes, held by a team from Livingstone & District AAC.

NOT THE SOUTHERN UPLAND WAY - A ROUTE

The Southern Uplands do give almost continuous hills from the North Sea to the Solway. It's a shame the SU Way doesn't!

Cocksburnspath to St. Mary's Loch
71 miles 8600 feet

A diversion north could be made through the Moorfoot Hills, sacrificing Galashiels Sewage Works for the sake of Oxton and Windlestraw Law. However, it takes an operatic composer of the calibre of Donizetti to make anything of the Lammermoors. A Walkman and the Sutherland/Pavarotti recording of 'Lucia di Lammermuir' may be the answer here.

The radical solution is to start at Lindisfarne; Hamish Brown's book *From the Pennines to the Highlands* guides between the Cheviots and Melrose. *The

Reivers' Way (James Roberts: Cicerone) or *Lakeland to Lindisfarne* (John Gillham: Crowood - a full colour hardback to be published Spring '95) gets you from the sea to the hills.

St. Mary's Loch to Beattock
21 Miles 3300 feet

Stay with the Southern Upland Way as it climbs to Pikestone Rig and then follow the ridge over Herman Law, Andrewhinney Hill and Bodesbeck Law to Capel Fell. Over Phawhope is just below, the first of five bothies you can use on the hundred miles to Glentrool. Rejoin the Southern Upland Way at Ettrick Head. (Do not go straight over to bag Wind Fell and Loch Fell. The narrow path through the pass is better.)

Beattock to Kettleton Byre Bothy
13 miles 3000 feet

Follow the SU Way's road (sorry!) all the way to Kinnelhead, then the track to Lochanhead. Climb Queensberry.

The rather scruffy bothy of Burleywhag is one and a half miles north west. Assuming you do not need it, cross Penbreck and follow the district boundary as it swings north to avoid steep broken ground and reach Earncraig and Gana Hills. Swing left to the conspicuous cairn of Garroch Fell, whence a short but sharp descent over heather gets you to a Landrover track. Follow this north-westwards to the first track junction, where you turn left on muddy wheelmarks to a cylindrical iron shed. Here another track starts up and takes you to Kettleton Byre bothy at GR 913020 (unnamed on my map). It's small but snug: if you want to light the stove bring your own fuel, chopped very short.

Wanlockhead, the highest village in Scotland. It is considerably higher and considerably more attractive than the highest village in the Highlands (Dalwhinnie: see Chapter 6)

Kettleton Byre to Wanlockhead
8 miles 4000 feet

Continue down the ancient and attractive track to Durisdeer, where the facilities are a cold-water tap, a phone box and an astonishing marble mausoleum in a lean-to behind the church. On Sunday afternoons in July, August or September you can get a home-baked Church Tea for £1.50.

Leave the village by the track to the right of the church. This is an old coach road to Edinburgh and, if you are in a hurry, you can swoop with it over the Well Pass to the A702 below Laight Hill and rejoin the regular Way. Alternatively leave it at the first gate on the left, cross Black and Well Hills and descend beside the waterfalls of the Lavern Burn. Scramble up the bed of the Dinabed Linn behind Upper Daveen to gain the Square Nick (unnamed at 892087). Descend to the Enterkin Burn. The path leading north is an even older road to Edinburgh, used by the retreating army of Bonny Prince Charlie. It leads to the Lowther Hill access road but you only have to use this for three hundred yards before the SU waymarks descend left to Wanlockhead.

N.B. In the reverse direction: from Wanlockhead follow the SU Way until it joins the tarred access road to the Civil Aviation Authority's domes. Turn right up the road for three hundred yards past a small grassy gully on the right, to where it turns 120 degrees left. You go straight ahead here on a path that initially is unclear. Power lines below can act as a guide for they rise to join the path.

Wanlockhead to Sanquhar
8 miles 1000 feet

The direct route over the grouse moors is one of the better bits of the SU Way. Parties without dogs who walk on the path and discreetly will do no harm during the grouse-nesting/lambing season. After August 12th, they do not shoot grouse on Sundays. On weekdays check with the factor's office at Drumlanrig Castle to see if they are shooting. The alternative route is a forest road with a view, which, I guess, is better than a forest road without one.

From Wanlockhead westwards you are in one of Scotland's depressed areas. Self reliance is a virtue but round here please spend your money. Sanquhar supermarket may not stock freeze-dried boeuf bourgignon but there's a choice of three butchers to get a haggis for that special bothy supper (serve it with instant mash).

Sanquhar to Carsphairn
21 miles 5200 feet

Follow the waymarks to the road bridge over the Euchan. Go up this river by the footpath on the north bank. Later, a track on the south bank to Glenmaddie lets you avoid much of the tarmac. Leave the road at the cattle grid above the filter station and climb right beside a small quarry then traverse Bank Hill - this avoids some silly business in the forest later on.

A damp, grassy ridge leads to Blacklorg Hill - don't use the alternative track and path by the Kello Glen to reach Afton, certainly not on weekdays. At Dunside they use dynamite to blast incompatible metals together and they do it right beside the track.

From Blacklorg continue north westwards to Craigbreanoch, which is the unnamed 575m lunch spot above the Afton Dam. Cross the dam. It has been built in the 1930's Odeon style and looks surprisingly good in it.

A track from the end of the dam doubles back onto the open hillside to let you cross Wedder Hill, Windy Standard and Dugland before dropping to the remote small bothy at Clennoch. This is even nicer than the one at Kettleton Byre. This time if you want to light the stove you will have to carry paraffin.

Between Clennoch and Cairnsmore you briefly leave the SU Way Map but all you have to do is ascend south west then south to the trig point. Descend by Black Shoulder and Dunool and then, if you do not want Willieanna, drop westwards onto a track to Green Well of Scotland.

Carsphairn no longer has an inn but it does have a useful village shop. A large bothy, surrounded by dripping fir trees, is at Shiel of Castlemaddy, three miles further; cross rough grassland by Cairn Avel and plunge into the gloomy trees at GR 554916.

Carsphairn to Bargennan
22 miles 4000 feet

The Galloway Hills are Southern Britain's third best range and to pass through them on a forest road is an unnecessary self-deprivation. This high-level route goes right through the middle.

Having positioned ourselves at Carsphairn, there's no way to avoid climbing Corserine. If you start from the bothy, take the forest road westward until you can see up a ride to the open hillside on your right. Take this and climb Cairnsgarroch. Otherwise take the track from Green Well of Scotland past Garryhorn to the disused mines and climb west to Coran of Portmark - this is off your SU Way map but it's at the north end of a very clear ridge at GR 509937. Follow the crest and fence southwards to Bow (back on the map) and Meaul. The cairn on Carlin's Cairn commemorates Robert the Bruce, who gave large grants of land to people who helped him "to be delivered after I'm King". What these particular helpers had done was to tie saucepans to their cattle and pretend they were an army. Peer over the escarpment on your left; it's a good place for wild goats.

From Corserine descend due west; a forest ride leads down to a forest road. The bothy at Backhill of Bush is two miles down the road on the left. Like Shiel of Castlemaddie and other forest bothies, there will usually be a pile of logs for firewood and even, if you are lucky, a saw and an axe.

Resisting these comforts, go straight over the road on your ride. Once out of the trees climb the valley between Dungeon Hill and Mullwarchar, walking on the rock of the stream bed if there's not too much water on it. Walk along

Loch Enoch, looking west to Redstone Rig. Galloway is the largest wild area outside the Highlands. A crossing of the Uplands will take one long day or two short ones with a bothy stop, and will pass the silver beaches of Loch Enoch. The Southern Upland Way on a forest road five miles to the south never even suspects its existence.

Waterproof granite means that the rain in Galloway stays there. Of the natural lochs in the Southern Uplands 91% are within 12 miles of Loch Enoch.

the eastern shores of Lochs Enoch and Neldricken on small, muddy paths. The going is slow, giving you plenty of time to enjoy the splendid surroundings. From the foot of Neldricken a well-trodden path leads down to Loch Trool. Turn left on the track towards Glenhead. After a mile Green Trail waymarks point right to a footbridge over Glenhead Burn and the SU Way.

It is a bad mistake to take the road down any part of Glentrool. The path south of the loch is awkward but interesting and the vertical bogs we encountered in 1986 have been carefully built over. The section below Caldons seldom floods in Summer and when it does is good fun in shorts and bare feet.

Bargennan to Portpatrick
40 miles 2000 feet

There are some nice bits and some of the nasty bits are gradually being eliminated by hard-working footpath rangers.

Chapter Six
THE WIDE WAY IN A WEEK
Ardnamurchan Point to Peterhead

"Don't go West to East and have all your fun at the beginning. Don't just do the eight highest mountains; do Garbh Bheinn and the Aonach Beag/Geal Charn ridge and the Fara and the Devil's Point and Ben Avon. And don't go all the way to Peterhead; you know what road-running does to your legs."

I give people advice even when they haven't paid for my book.

"Well," Glyn conceded, "Maybe I'll take in Ben Resipol."

On a cool and showery Saturday morning in late May he hitched to the westernmost point of the Scottish landmass - a draughty spot on the Ardnamurchan Peninsular where there are quite a lot of seals but not many humans.

Research in Dumfries Library (my research; during lambing Glyn doesn't have time for libraries) showed that three or four of Hamish MacInnes' *West Highland Walks* did bits of Ardnamurchan's north shore so that was the way he went to Archaracle. "Friendly bog," he wrote, "no Galloway tussocks!"

He travelled light and hoped to travel fast - 40 miles or so in a day and across in a week. There wasn't much in the little nylon rucksack. (15lb, excluding food: see Chapter 9.) His usual silage bag had been replaced by the orange plastic one I picked up on the Southern Upland Way: very similar performance but the safety instructions printed on it gave him some reading matter for the evenings. Several thin layers are better than one thick one: Glyn's layers were thin, even when new. Now they are very thin indeed.

We want our gear to be cheap, lightweight, comfortable and stylish. But apart from the naked skin we're born with, nothing is all four. If, however, you ignore the last two variables, as Glyn does, then there's the ultimate windproof undergarment: the bin-liner with three holes in. None of this takes up much space and his sleeping bag is not terribly big so it was the mass of junk food crammed in the top that split the rucksack down the back seam. (Glyn's high-speed, long-distance diet is based on custard cream biscuits.)

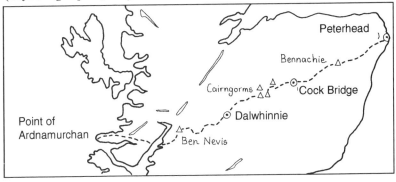

This was to turn out less serious than it seemed... severe food shortages over the rest of the trip would at least relieve the strain on the sack.

He climbed over Ben Resipol, revelling in the space and emptiness and imagining jagged Cuillin across twenty miles of sparkling water. But grey mist from Sgurr Dhomhnuill looks much the same as from Ben Resipol. A crucial resupply point was ahead so he pounded down Glen Gour, reaching the shop at Clovullin with fifteen minutes to spare before 5.00 closing time.

Now the day after Saturday is, unfortunately, a Sunday. On a Sunday the shop closes at 4.30. In a less civilised spot, such as London or Edinburgh, this would be a problem. But in the Western Highlands you just stand looking sad for a minute or two and a kind lady will come and re-open the shop.

Glyn trailed off up the forest trail with the waterfalls and into the dripping forest of Glen Righ. With some relief he found as night fell a small trackside

Glyn, in front, and the author in Glen Nevis, starting a 60-mile hill run. Taking on more than you think you can finish adds to the excitement; a properly-equipped walker need not fear the involuntary night out. (Note that our 15lb rucksacks are doing the initial road section by car.)   *Photo: Peter Trenchard*

shack. It wasn't a very nice shack but at least the roof kept out some of the rain and the door, some of the midges. It was too dark to see the pile of human ordure in the corner (with the used paper neatly pressed into the top). He saw that in the morning.

The hills remain free for all and this must include obnoxious and selfish people along with the nice ones. One day they'll start charging us for clearing up after these people. And once these people are having to pay they'll feel even more entitled to scatter their litter. Ah well: Everest's about £7,000 these days, which makes £100 each for Munros look quite a bargain considering Everest's a three-day snow plod and a fortnight at Base Camp with altitude sickness.

But let us turn to pleasanter subjects such as Mullach nan Coirean on the end of the Mamores and the Carn Mor Dearg Arete. It's hard to be alone on Ben Nevis; you could do it by climbing Point Five Gully in high Summer perhaps, and Glyn managed it with his approach over Carn Dearg. Actually Ben Nevis has five outliers, all called Carn Dearg. The name means "pile of stones, reddish grey in colour" and this south-western one lives up to the description, being the tallest slope of heather-covered, jammed rocks in Great Britain.

"Interesting," said Glyn afterwards: "any steeper and the whole lot would end up in Glen Nevis." Glyn too, of course; but we don't mention that. We hill runners pride ourselves on enjoying challenging bits of ground.

You can't do the Carn Mor Dearg Arete too often; each time different bits of Nevis' terrific northern crags appear through the gaps in the cloud. There are other days, though, when you see no crags but hear them as a roaring in the distant mist: when rain off the pinnacles drips upwards in the wind that bursts out of Corrie Leis. On those days, to be alone in lightweight running gear on Scotland's biggest hill is to be very small indeed.

A runner's comfort and his first line of safety is his confidence that he can get off the hill fast. The second line is the stuff in his sack, which is sufficient to assure survival: but survival in such extreme discomfort as hardly to bear thinking about. Extra fitness is not of course enough to make the average hill-runner as safe as the average hill-walker; the extra risk is justified by (we assert this with an absolutely straight face and how do you know if you haven't tried?) extra pleasure.

With the odd Mamore on the start of a wet day, time was running out and so too after the Aonachs did Glyn - to the bothy marked Luibeilt on the map. It's actually called Meanach, the unnamed building off the path 300m east of Luibeilt. His day of 22 miles and 10,000 feet had been, in hill-running terms, a short one; wind, slippery rocks and rain on his glasses had slowed him down.

The next day the cloud was low and so were the supplies. He ran around the bottoms of a dozen of Scotland's finest mountains, along the shores of Loch Treig and Loch Ossian. The Beallach Dubh - the sinister Black Pass - climbs a heathery path to nearly 2500 feet. It's a place of little rocky streams, clamped between thousand foot grass walls. A wide empty valley leads down to the Landrover track along Loch Ericht. Glyn reached the shop at

Dalwhinnie with an hour to spare. Unfortunately there isn't a shop at Dalwhinnie.

No amount of standing around looking sad was going to help with this one. The kind lady (I've an idea her name was Mrs Macpherson) who has helped so many long-distance walkers and would have helped Glyn, had died two months earlier.

Even today Glyn cannot pass through Dalwhinnie, an austere spot at the best of times, without a shudder. As he left it on that May evening, grey clouds were skimming the black surface of the A9. In his belly he carried a high grease snack from the transport café: on his back a 1kg bag of white sugar, six Mars bars and just half a loaf of sliced bread for the sixty-mile crossing through Britain's most demanding mountain range. (He refused their milk. He's used to fresh milk from his own cow and didn't see any point in spending money on semi-skimmed. "Basically just water. Get that from a stream.")

Satellite-linked navigation systems cost only £1000 and tell you where you are to within 200 metres. In another ten years they will call us irresponsible fools if we don't carry one - and then where will be the fun on the Great Moss in the mist? Hitting the Pools of Dee after a 3½ mile compass bearing gave him particular pleasure: the longest compass-bearing of his life so far and all done at an altitude of three and a half thousand feet.

What's it all about? Sir Hugh Munro thought up a good game with his 277 mountains over 3000 feet but it isn't Glyn's game and he has already run past sixteen Munros to get to biscuits. But despite the now fairly serious biscuit situation, the night at Shelter Stone is part of his game, so after his four-thousanders he must double back around the head of Loch Avon and look for the big rock with the cairn on the top.

On this fifth day of his trip the weather has been less cruel with rain more-or-less vertical instead of straight at the specs. He has achieved his first real runners' day. Over thirty miles and 10,000 feet say a lot for the lifting power of sugar and white bread.

The hole under Shelter Stone is dirty and dark. The ceiling is low and so is the temperature. There are mice. Even when it isn't snowing outside, it is quite simply the most romantic bedroom in Britain.

The sixth day dawned like others - grey and wet. Glyn found some scraps at Fords of Avon bothy and public spiritedly, to discourage bothy mice, ate them. There was still plenty of sugar; pure sucrose was proving difficult to eat. His rucksack was held together with binder-twine and his almost new running shoes were falling apart as his feet swelled inside them. The most straightforward route out was called for and for once Glyn heeded the call. The two fine Munros to the south were saved for the future as he strode out along the bottom of Glen Avon.

"Striding?" This is a technical hill-running term meaning - well -walking, actually.

Lost people in the Cairngorms occasionally decide to follow the river down from Loch Avon to Civilisation. The theory is sound; the river is a big one, the valley floor is flat and necessarily downhill. But the practice is hard. The first inhabited house is twenty miles downstream. He emerged from the hills at 7.00pm after five days and three hours of travel. He phoned in to learn that Peter, his control, had got a bit anxious about the one bag of sugar across the Cairngorms and was up in Aberdeenshire looking for him. "Well he'll have trouble finding me," said Glyn. "I'm not sticking around here for long." Cock Bridge has a hotel but no shop. Glyn bought some peanuts in the bar and set off over the moss, licking the last of the sugar from the bottom of the bag. The coast was only sixty-six miles of lowland away; by walking through the night and running through the day he should be in time for a late supper.

The supper was going to be a very late one indeed. He slept on the moors, reached a shop and plodded on at an ever-decreasing pace on little country lanes and the old tracks marked on Bartholemew's maps, some of which existed in real life. Perhaps by this time he was beginning to wonder if he himself existed in real life. He spent his seventh night on Bennachie. At 1733 feet Bennachie is a fine small bedroom with a song about it ("At the back of Bennachie") and a hill race up it every September. The Cairngorms, a line of humps against the sunset, looked a long way back, and the sunrise flashed off the North Sea. If he could reach that by 4.00pm he'd have his crossing-in-a-week.

Peter finally caught up with him on the lane behind Oldmeldrum. "Anything I can do? Take the sack for a few miles?"

No; the sack, collapsing but indomitable, was determined to finish the walk under its own power. The shoes, however, were just about ready to chuck it in.

"You could buy me a pair of wellies. They'll need plenty of extra space for these blisters; better make them elevens."

Peter got the last pair of elevens in Oldmeldrum. Then he went for a run on Bennachie: nice hill, but a long way to come back in September for a sixty-minute race. The 4.00pm deadline passed unnoticed in the pain. But at last, the road grew a pavement with other people walking on it. The houses closed in around them; they turned the corner and saw the masts of the fishing fleet and heard the cry of the gulls. At ten minutes before midnight they walked out along the pier to the easternmost point of Scotland.

Day No.	Stage (from-to)	distance miles	climb feet	time hours
1	Ardnamurchan Point - Acharacle	24	2,200	7
2	Archaracle - Glen Righ	31	4,200	12
3	Glen Righ - Luibeilt	22	9,500	14
4	Luibeilt - Loch Cuaich	39	2,500	12½
5	Loch Cuaich - Shelter Stone	30	9,000	16
6	Shelter Stone - Craig of Bunzeoch	28	1,000	13
7	Craig of Bunzeoch - Bennachie	28	3,300	12
8	Bennachie - Peterhead	38	1,300	15
	TOTAL	240	30,000	7days 7hr

Afterthought To Chapter 6

The Grey Corries To Ben Nevis

This terrific ridge of the Grey Corries and Aonachs will be the high point of many coast-to-coasts - well, any higher than Ben Nevis and you would have to be a bird.

From the cosy bothy of Lairig Leacach it's 16 miles and 8,000 steep feet to Glen Nevis, first along the shattered quartzite crest, then a drop to 2,500 feet and onto the stony plateau of the Aonachs. Care is needed coming westwards off Aonach Mor; a small cairn on the plateau's edge marks the top of the spur down to the col. All this is a fitting prelude to the rocky crest of the Carn Mor Dearg Arete, where your cries of terror will be thrown back at you by the vast crags of Nevis across the corrie.

The difficulties, such as they are, of the Arete can be avoided on the south side, but if there's fresh snow or frozen ground, the firm rock of the crest is preferable to the treacheries of the path.

Coming the other way there's an extra 1500 feet to climb getting out of Ben Nevis. Members of the Scottish Mountaineering Club and their guests can start from the comforts of the CIC Hut; others might camp at Lochan Meall an-t-Suidhe (Melantee) or the grim hovel on the summit of Ben Nevis itself. The tricky bit is coming off Aonach Beag. Dive confidently off the side of the ridge at GR 207707, just south of the little top where it changes direction from east to south. A tiny but visible path leads down the crest of a small spur. A full day for anyone......well, almost anyone.....runners will consider how close their time from Glen Nevis to the bothy is to the 6hrs 25mins they'll need if they are to achieve Charlie Ramsay's Round of 24 Lochaber Munros in 24 hours.

Chapter 7
ABSURDLY ROMANTIC MULL
A Four-day Coast-to-Coast Crossing of the Island

The Ross of Mull, which I had now got upon was rugged and trackless, like the isle (Erraid) I had just left; being all bog, and brier and big stone....

Kidnapped by Robert Louis Stevenson

In fiction something exciting happens on every page, in biography, usually, not. Here on the Isle of Mull, though, such distinctions blur and disappear like the waves of the surrounding sea. History and current affairs become hopelessly entangled and real life floats like mountaintops glimpsed through the mist of dreams.

On this crossing you will walk through the sea and across the tops of the clouds. Cliffs, caves and the ghosts of murdered MacLeans will haunt your crossing. Eagles, wild goats and horseflies will be your companions. Stevenson's comments are still apt. There are few paths and many rocks; it'll take longer than you think.

An unmurdered MacLean was my companion on Mull, though himself from the South London branch of the clan. This was his first long-distance walk but at least he had the right idea: his idea was that we should bivouac on the summit of Ben More.

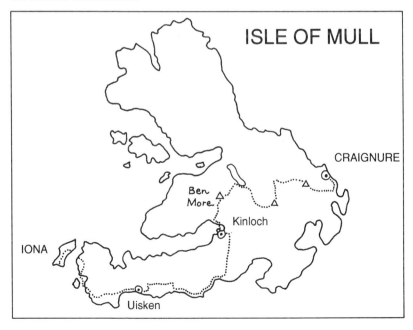

Day 1: Iona to Uisken
12 miles 1000 ft

The start of the walk is at Coracle Bay (Port na Curaich) at the southern end of Iona. A small path winds inland between the ancient rocks past the pond of Loch Staoinaig and the golf course. (The spouting cave is worth a diversion in a south-westerly.) Take the small road eastwards and the track on the left through Maol farm to the ruins of the nunnery and to the ferry.

At Coracle Bay Columba first touched British soil; it's green, circled by rocks and you may find garnets on the beach. If you don't have a coracle of your own, you will find a boatman to sail you across in the listings at the end of this chapter.

> "That man is little to be envied whose piety would not grow warmer among the ruins of Iona," says Dr Johnson.

Linger for a while; wonder with Columba what dangers lie ahead, how terrible the sufferings are likely to be and how slight the rewards. Are the residents civilised? Will there be anywhere to get a hot meal? Have they started building Edinburgh yet?

We did our lingering on Dun I (pronounced 'ee"). There we met a disgruntled diver who said his piety had been in no way been warmed up by barefoot hippies dancing in circles. No doubt Columba himself was considered a dangerous nutter and the Irish were probably glad enough to have him clear off in his Coracle to bother the Scots. The Abbey itself is an impressive modern reconstruction but I prefer Dun I, even though it doesn't have an Interpretion Centre where you can see it all on video in case real life should be too strong for you. All over Britain the Historic Monument is being reduced to the same pre-digested experience: a place to watch low-budget television considerably worse than anything on your screen at home, but where you can be reasonably sure of getting a cup of decent coffee.

At the edges of the island though, at the ends of the day, Iona is a place to linger. We had to come back after our walk to do our lingering on Iona. I'd neglected to hire a proper boatman, neglected the fact that it was Sunday with no early boat, and found myself running from the pier to Coracle Bay and back between ferries in an hour and two minutes. The beauties of Iona cannot really be appreciated at such a speed .

Visitors are not allowed to drive onto the island. Why then is the ferry to Fionnphort a steel bucket resembling a building-site skip designed to carry cars? The crossing of the narrow sound of Iona spans three billion years, which is roughly two thirds of the lifetime of the planet, half of the lifetime of the Solar System, a fifth of the lifetime of the Universe so far. The rocks of Iona are of the Lewisian Gneiss, one of the oldest stones in the world. The pink granite of the Ross of Mull is positively new-grown, a mere fifty million years old.

Fionnphort ("Finnyfort") means "beautiful port" and though it's a scruffy tourist village the name is correct; to sailors it's the best place they'll ever see.

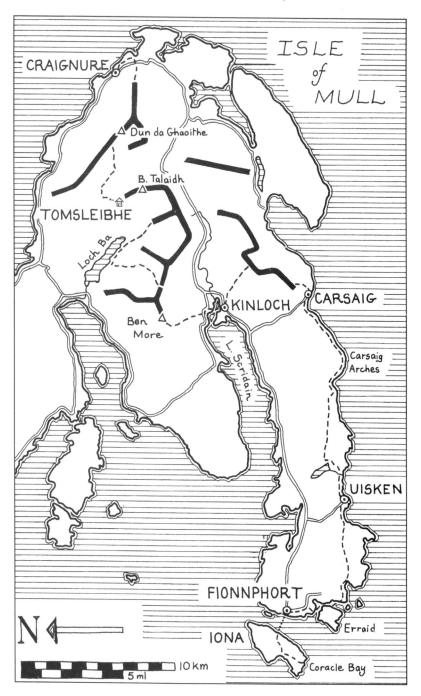

ISLE of MULL

CRAIGNURE

△ Dun da Ghaoithe

B. Talaidh △

TOMSLEIBHE

Loch Ba

Ben More △

KINLOCH

CARSAIG

L. Scridain

Carsaig Arches

UISKEN

FIONNPHORT

N◄

IONA

Erraid

Coracle Bay

10 km

5 ml

The ford at Kinloch is one of the absurd moments on Absurdly Romantic Mull. Although we are below sea level, the paddling is through the fresh water of the Coladoir river as it spreads across the foreshore.

Two other sailing grounds are almost as good as these Western Isles: the seas around Greece and the Great Barrier Reef.

The MacLean left me here to try and find himself some of this boating fun. He would rejoin the expedition after Carsaig Arches, provided I managed to get to Carsaig Arches. There would be, he promised, no way down through the cliffs west of the Arches; and once having not got down through the cliffs, the sea would prevent any progress along the foreshore.

But if Davie Balfour managed it in four days, and him but a fictional character, then so should we. If like Davie, you are lucky enough to have an evil uncle outside Edinburgh, he will have arranged for you to have been shipwrecked on the Torran Rocks and washed ashore on Erraid. Robert Louis Stevenson's hero Davie Balfour started his coast-to-coast here, finishing after various adventures at Queensferry on the Forth. Foreign readers of English literature rate Stevenson as one of the finest writers of the language. They have the difficulties of translation to contend with; perhaps for us he is simply too enjoyable to be really great. In which case must the same be said for this walk inspired by the seventh chapter of *Kidnapped*?

Take the road to Fidden Farm and the track left of the caravan field to the beach opposite the island of Erraid. The causeway to Erraid is only passable for an hour or so either side of high tide (six minutes later than Oban's). If you cross before low water you should have no trouble with the return crossing of the Erraid Sound as its yellow sands remain uncovered for rather longer. Around high tide though it will be best to omit Erraid altogether, leave the beach at Cul-a-Bhaile and take the small road to Knockvologan farm. A track leads back to the sand.

These perfect beaches look across a sea of gleaming green to a multitude of islands. In my running shoes and rucksack I startled occasional bathers, the human ones as much as the seals. I left the sand at GR 308193 to cross south-east. The going here consists of outcrops and grassy hollows dipping into the next bay of Port nan Ron. The circuit of this bay is at low tide a sandy stroll; at high tide though the choice is between scrambles around the low cliffs or hacking through waist-high woodland of birch and oak. Rock cracks run back into the moor; often you will turn left when you should turn right, or jump one only to find a larger immediately beyond. The association was hard to pin because the colours were all wrong, but paint the whole thing white and you're crevasse-hopping on an Alpine Glacier; and it's all too easy to become hopping mad...

Leave the sea at Bagh Tir Chille and pass across the moor by Lochs Cholarich, an Sgalain and Mor Ardalanish. The shallow boggy valleys are grassy, but the grass is long and mixed with Bog Myrtle that's gentle on the nose but hard on the legs. Often you are crossing the raised ridges of former cultivation. This was formerly rich and cultivated land, and the settlement at Tir Fhearagain ("Chirr-Irrigin") was large enough to support a school. But I was still thinking glaciers, and these open vales gathered heat and moisture like a glacier in the still afternoon; oddly, an afternoon glacier is oppressively hot and you plod through slushy snow that gets your feet as wet as any Scottish bog.

Cross the wide sands of Ardalanish. At the bay's eastern corner, climb Aird Dubh by a rocky rib that overhangs on the left but has a sheep path along the crest.

The beach at Uisken was covered in human beings; I'd arrived in the middle of the Uisken Games (last Sunday in July). It would be most unsporting

to pass without participating, and I was just in time for the Iona Ferry Race...
Carl Gustav Jung would have been pleased to note that after a lifetime without any Iona Ferry Race I was now about to participate in, yes, two separate
ones in a single day. Marvelling on the mysteries of Synchronicity I formed
myself into a team with an instant stranger and collected the race kit of a
fishcrate, three floats and two small children. We came a triumphant second.

Day 2 Uisken to Kinloch
19 miles 3000 ft

A small sea-bather's path leaves the corner of the beach to gain the next two
bays. Dun a Geard displays the whole coast behind as well as some mysterious stonework. Leave the shore on the northward track and enter the forest
beside Loch Assipol.

The forest track is dull but it doesn't do to let the young people get too
excited, and there's some stuff ahead that needs to be approached in a calm
frame of mind. At the end of the track turn right to a small standing stone
(GR 462199) where local singers pose above the semi-infinite sea view for
the covers of their cassettes. This stone is one of a series leading to Iona from
Grass Point at the SE corner of the island: perhaps the earliest example of a
waymarked long-distance trail. Pilgrims were supposed to see each one from
the one before but, as on more recent paths, the markers are too far apart to
be useful in mist when you need them most.

Descend beside the stream (deer path) and along the deer fence. Climb the
fence carefully at the corner pole with two supporters. This pole is half way
between two streams (GR 465195). Just at this point it is easy to descend
through the upper line of cliffs on grass. Elsewhere it isn't!

"Er... excuse me Gerald, but what's that peculiar object bouncing about on
the top of the bracken?"

"Why bless my antlers... it looks like... it is the top bit of a human being.
And it's coming down! Hey, George! We're moving off a bit! George!"

But George, head down in the bracken, didn't hear their barks, and two
minutes later I was treated to the sudden sight of the ears and head of a
young deer bouncing away in front of me like a football I'd just kicked.

Progress eastward along the shore is blocked by cliffs descending into the
sea. Traverse east above these lower cliffs through a large herd of wild goats
which delight in posing on the brinks of the various available abysses. It is
said that the goats came on the Spanish Armada and what harm can be done
by believing this...

The cliffs below force you ever higher but eventually you emerge on flat
ground at the top of a narrow gullet between the cliffs. This grassy gullet at
GR 475196 gives a spectacular descent on a small zig-zag path. The path
enters the gullet at its NE corner and nowhere requires the use of the hands;
if you need to you are probably in the wrong place and may be in

considerable danger. If you fail to find the descent, then continue eastward for three miles above the cliffs to descend by the Nun's Pass.

Having found the descent, continue along the shore on narrow paths. At two points the driftwood just reaches the foot of the cliff and if the tide is very high you may have to wait for an hour or two: no great imposition in these spectacular surroundings. The view southward towards Jura, Colonsay and Islay is very good but the view vertically upwards is even finer. Here we saw buzzards being mobbed by blackbirds... wait a minute: blackbirds don't mob birds of prey. Those blackbirds must be ravens, and the buzzards are of course eagles. The principle difference between a buzzard and an eagle is that the eagle is much further away.

A clansman called Gorrie registered his protest against an oppressive chieftain by leaping off these cliffs with the chieftain's infant son in his arms.

It's at Carsaig Arches that you realise that this route really is too good to be true. The path becomes particularly exciting above the second arch, with thrilling precipices at its right-hand side. It continues along the shore, constantly dodging around rock obstacles. Where it crosses a recent landslip it reminded me so forcefully of an alpine moraine that I started looking for red-and-white marker flashes on the rocks... in truth I was by this time a little tired, or perhaps simply over-excited.

The Nun's Cave (524204) is an admirable bivvy with space for about 40. The floor of dried powdered goat dung will require some plastic sheeting, and fresh water is not terribly handy so bring a large container. The cave is just above the path but concealed from it by a mound of rock and earth; start looking for it after the large waterfall. Nuns hid here after being thrown off Iona by the Vikings and have carved various decorations into the walls. So, alas, have later visitors.

Apart from the cave and a phone box, the settlement of Carsaig has no useful facilities. From its easternmost building climb through steep wood NE, then north onto Ben Charsaig. The high, grassy moor beyond has intricate, detailed views if the cloud is up: intricate, detailed navigation if it isn't. Enter the forest at its easternmost corner below Beinn nam Feannag.

An indistinct old path, which started at Glenbyre, leads through a gap in the trees to join the forest track at its crossing of the Allt a Mhaim. Here there fell on our heads quite suddenly about half an inch of rain, which is roughly a bucketful each. The stream became a roaring whitewater streak; canoes and a great deal of courage would have given us an unprecedented descent to the hotel. We preferred a sodden plod. The hill opposite was as usual Less rather than More, being quite invisible inside its cloud.

Day 3: Ben More to Tomsleibhe Bothy
17 miles 6500ft

Sixty million years ago Scotland was out in the Atlantic and sitting on top of the Mid-Atlantic Rift, the way Iceland is today. Like Iceland now, Scotland then had volcanoes in a line running north and south. Skye and

Ardnamurchan were two of them, Arran was another. But the greatest of them was on Mull. Dykes from the Mull volcano - underground lavas forced along weakness in the pre-existing rocks - extend to Inverness and Northern England, and Ben More was the highest point in Northern Europe.

At 3169 feet it's rather high even now: specially when your ascent starts from below sea level. A sea-stained post opposite the Kinloch Hotel marks the start of the crossing of the gravel of An Leth-onn and there is another post half-way across. This old ford passes along the eastern edge of a spit of land to join the road at GR 535290. There's a lot of water to cross but none of it is more than knee-deep - unless the tide's in!

Climb Ben More by its southern shoulder. Above Maol nan Damh is much small scree, which is pleasant in descent, tiresome going up. Ben More has some magnetic rock which extends to A'Chioch; if you are aware of this it should not be a problem. Don't take bearings inside the circular summit cairn and don't hold your compass beside any suspicious-looking reddish boulders. On the summit scree you can take a reliable bearing for the ridge to A'Chioch.

The ridge from Ben More to A'Chioch is a fine and spectacular scramble. Difficulties can (but of course shouldn't) be avoided on small paths to the right (South). The climbing too is a few feet south of the crest. While there are vertical views down the north side through gaps in the crest, the harder bits of rock have comforting ledges below. The rock is sound and, on the correct line, clean; the grade is One.

Because of the MacLean's commendable desire to bivouac on the summit, we were doing this part of the route in reverse. Climbing into thick mist at 2000 ft at seven in the evening is not altogether sensible, specially when the thick mist contains a rocky and possibly dangerous ridge...

So it is cruelly unfair on the people who'd have taken the foul weather alternative that, as we reached A'Chioch's narrow summit, the mist had decided it had had enough and collapsed wearily into the valleys. Abandoning our expectations of a memorably unpleasant night huddled between wet boulders, we settled down for an hour or two and watched the departing clouds curl among the turrets of the Ben More ridge and flow like water over the cols below.

The ascent of the ridge was slow in the fading daylight: not because of any steepness or dificulty, but because of frequent stops for photographs.

Dr Johnson's idea of paradise was to eat caviar to the sound of trumpets, and the visual equivalent of the trumpets was our final summit view of distant Atlantic and distant mainland peaks, while stray shafts of pink picked single islands from the grey sea. Lighthouses came out like stars and winked at us, and the Outer Isles swung like ghost ships along the horizon. The food, however, was not caviar but instant mash (although the exotic type with dried onion and country herbs) and to be eating this with a plastic spoon among such splendour was silly enough to make me giggle.

A few midges came out and danced around the remains of the trig point; so we could be sure that, at that moment, no point on the island was free of the little things. Of course the only place to bivvy down was along the summit

The summit of Ben More, looking back across Iona into the Atlantic. (Such late evening views are the reward for the starlit bivouac. The camera has trouble recording these grey-on-grey scenes; the human brain will do a much better job.

stones, and of course it rained before morning. We'd have been disappointed if it hadn't.

As elsewhere in Scotland, "Cioch" means the breast of a woman, but if you want a more chaste translation it is also "limpet". Descend the frightful boulderslope south-east - it's nastier than Skye's Great Stoneshoot or the quartzite of Stob Ban in the Grey Corries. The cairn in the 332m col marks the boundary of the ancient kingdoms of Scotland and Dalriada, and there's still a certain coolness between those of North Mull and the South. The compensation for the nasty boulders is the ancient descent into Glen Clachaig.

"It's as big as Upper Ennerdale", the MacLean points out. But here is only a single path and just two people: and swooping green hillsides with grey crags towering into the cloud. Turn right at Loch Ba and take the track through remnants of hazel and oak to Gortenbuie.

The burial ground here was ploughed under at the time of the Clearances to prevent the islanders from returning to visit the graves. There's a footbridge on the join of the maps at 600345 which will be of service to those omitting the day's final hills. The rest of us climb Beinn Chaisgidle. Oddly, this is the centre of the former volcano; once a place of fire and ash, it now consists of peat and little pools. Follow the grassy and undemanding ridge round by Sgulan Mor to Beinn Talaidh (2505 ft).

The remains of a wartime Dakota can be found in the headwaters of the Allt nan Clar. Coming from Canada in February 1945, it became heavily iced and clipped the summit to slide down the northern slopes. Astonishingly, four of the seven on board survived.

The bothy vandals find Tomsleibhe too far to come, and you should find it clean, midge-proof and with dry kindling to hand. A waterfall supplies your washbasin, which is shaded by birch and mountain ash.

High Tide Alternative: it's only two miles further by the bridge.
Foul Weather Alternative: Ancient path from Ardvergnish to Loch Ba; Glen Cannel; East slopes of Beinn na Duatharach.

Day 4: Tomsleibhe to Craignure
11 miles 2700 ft

A shorter final day leaves time for visits to Duart and Torosay Castles, a ride on the little railway or an early ferry to Oban.

The land marked as being under FC ownership in Glen Forsa is now also under trees. Electric deer fences preclude short-cuts. Take the track north, even as far as the bridge if the river is too full. Helpful wheelmarks run along the north-eastern edge of the trees past the ruin at Rhoall.

Steep slopes climb rapidly out of the forest. It's a green and peaceful place; it's hard to believe that the ice-creams and picture postcards of Craignure are less than five miles away behind the ridge.

Ascend the long grassy rib of Beinn Thunicaraidh and the stony slopes to Dun da Ghaoithe. This is the "Fort of the Winds"; the Gaelic word also appears in the name of Goatfell on Arran. The Dun is the second and better of Mull's Corbetts and the views, if you can see any, are wonderful. It has a large rounded cairn, but after the mile of airy ridge to Mannir nam Fiadh is an even larger one as well as a cylindrical trig point. Only Tinto Hill in Lanarkshire has a larger cairn than Mannir nam Fiadh and, without any particular reason, I suppose it to have been started in the Bronze Age.

Descend gently eastward to the mast at Maol nan Uan and Torosay Castle, and follow the track beside the railway to the little port of Craignure. Craignure has beer and busses but lacks the atmosphere of Coracle Bay. Maybe, though, it's only a staging point as you follow Davie Balfour towards Queensferry, St Aidan towards Lindisfarne or Chapter 3 for the Abbey at Arbroath.

And what of the MacLean? When last I heard he was just off up Ben More to bivouac on the summit again. The midges of Mull bite deep but Ben More bites deeper.

DATA FILE

Distance & climb:	60 miles 13000 ft 4 days
Terrain:	Roadless and mostly pathless. The coastal walking will be found more demanding than mere distance would suggest.
Style, Equipment:	Cave at Carsaig and bothy at Tomsleibhe mean tent should be unnecessary. Bivvy bag, of course. There are no regular mountain rescue services on Mull.
Maps:	O.S. Landranger Nos 48 & 49
Direction:	I like to have the flat bit at the beginning, and Coracle Bay is a romantic start. However, you may well prefer to do the Cioch - Ben More ridge uphill.

Transport
to Oban	Several trains and busses from Glasgow daily ferry (MacBrayne's) every two hours to Craignure
to Fionnphort	Two busses a day, connecting with one morning and one late-afternoon ferry.
to Iona	Ferries are frequent on weekdays, hourly on Sundays
to Corracle Bay	The proper way.: Alternative Boat Hire Tel 016817 537

Accommodation and shops
Iona	Hotels, B&B, shops (closed Sunday)
Fionnphort	Hotel, B&B, shops
Erraid Bay	Campsite at Fidden Farm
	B&B at Cul a Bhaile
Uisken	B&B at Uisken Croft (Mrs Campbell 016817 307); camping permission
Bunessan (2 miles north of route)	
	All facilities
Carsaig	Cave, phone box only
Kinloch (head of Loch Scridain)	
	Kinloch Hotel (016814 204)
	B&B Tigh na-h-Abhann {016814 229)
	Small shop
Tomsleibhe	Bothy
Craignure	all facilities

Access
	Deer stalking affects whole route east of Carsaig from end August - end October.

Tourist Information
	Oban 01631 63122
	Tobermory 01688 2182
(bus timetables, ferry timetables, accommodation, stalking)	

Guidebook	Walking in South Mull & Iona (Brown & Whittaker) Oban Times PO Box 1, Oban: revised 1993) Cheap and good.

Looking across the three billion year gap from Iona to the Ross of Mull. (Advance planning pays dividends here; arranging for a real boat to carry you to Coracle Bay will increase still further the romance of Absurdly Romantic Mull.

CHAPTER 8

STYLE AND ACCOMMODATION

In crossing Scotland, as in real life, there are various ways of going about the thing. You do not pass a quantity surveyor in the street and say, "that man has got it all wrong. He ought to be a chartered accountant." There are, however, those who'll tell you that you shouldn't sneak from hotel to warm hotel: you ought to be doing it with a tent. What they mean is that they carried 30lb (15kg) all the way and they do not see why you should get away with 15lb (8kg).

The big disadvantage of hotels is that they make you eat your breakfast about three hours too late. This is outweighed by their great advantage, which is that you get to wash your socks.

My own preferred style, the way we did the "Summits of the South", is to use every one of the different types of accommodation, with a warm roof every three days. The load on the back is never completely unbearable, the widest chunks of empty country may be crossed and the delights of the hotel, when finally reached, are enjoyed to the full.

Hotel

It is quite possible to devise a route with no more than 15 miles a day and a warm bed at the end of it. (Hamish Brown's book - see Bibliography - describes such a route.) So why don't we all go out and buy ourselves a nice, small rucksack and do just that?

Well firstly, it does limit your choice of routes. There's no accommodation on the Great Moss. Secondly: it restricts you in time as well as space. If you are walking without a tent you will need to book your bed and, in some places, booking the night's bed in the morning isn't soon enough. This means a schedule and sticking to that schedule even though the bite of the heather's got into your legs and you feel like doing two days at a time. If you are carrying a tent or can bear to sleep in your bivvy bag, then booking becomes less crucial.

    Book yourself into :-
        very small places
        hotels in the middle of nowhere (Tomdoun, Cock Bridge)
        the far West, especially on the coast.
        places on the West Highland Way.

Tell them you are arriving on foot; you may find them less unsympathetic than you would expect when you turn up soaking wet and two days late. Exhaustive personal investigation has failed to discover a nasty hotel though there's a rumour of a place in Brechin.... The very cheap ones have showers; the expensive ones have tight little en suite bathrooms; the ones at £20 have

Lochan Rath: idyllic high camping at the end of the Grey Corries. The author has just run out of energy on the 24-hour Ramsay Round circuit and is preparing to bivvi down while the rest of the World is waking up.   *Photo: Peter Trenchard*

a massive tub with brass taps at the end of the passage.

B&B's
They fill up quicker than hotels. I have not listed them because they come and go - use research methods in Chapter 11.

Bunkhouses
Many walkers' hotels have a bunkhouse with a wooden shelf and some foam rubber where you unroll your sleeping bag. They charge about a £5 per night. Advantage: you can cook your own breakfast and leave at 7 o' clock. Disadvantage: you have to carry a sleeping bag.

Youth Hostel
About £8 (1994) for the more mature sort of youth plus £5 to join the SYHA, and in Scotland you still do your own cooking and sweeping up. In the more romantic ones (Glen Affric, Loch Ossian) and in climbing areas (Glenbrittle, Glencoe) you will need to book. In forgotten country towns (Ballater, Killin) you will not. If you have booked you must arrive by 6.00pm or you may find someone else in your bed.

Bothy
A bothy is a simple shelter not on a road. It has no lock, no warden and no charge. It also lacks electricity and running water. It will have a fireplace and a wooden platform to sleep on. Many are maintained by the Mountain

Bothies Association and if you join you will get their list. Many are marked on the maps; a few you will hear about from friends. Bothies are one of the reasons that Scotland's the best walking country in the World.

Tent

A little green tent for two (David and I use the 1 1/2 man size but we're neither of us much more than three quarters) weighs about 4lb (2kg). It is the sleeping bag, the cooker, the pans, the 3 day's food and the extra dry clothes for the night that haul the sack up to over 30lb (13kg). For those prepared to take up this burden, the rewards are great: wind and sleet at 3500 ft on the Great Moss or a midge-infested bog on Skye. Well you have to suffer if you want to have fun.

Bivvy Bag

Your bivvy bag is your emergency fall-back for when your leg breaks, or when you didn't bother to book, or the bothy has burnt down. You're not meant to enjoy it and if it's an orange plastic one or Glyn's silage bag you will not. The modern green breathable sort, though, is an option for those who find a tent too much like ordinary town life. Goretex ones cost over £100 - mine (Katmandu Trekking) was £30, I don't know why.

With a green breathable bag and a not-too-heavy sleeping bag to go inside it, you are ready to climb the   wobbly stepladder into a new realm of suffering and delight. This is the..........

Starlit night out

You only do this if the weather and the weather forecast are good. You walk to your mountain top, slowly so as not to get sweaty, arriving quarter of an hour before sunset. You put on all your clothes, the emergency socks, the smart hotel shirt, the waterproofs (if breathable) and get into the bag. You watch the sunset.

Fumbling with the cooker in the chill night air isn't worth it; eat cold food - smoked chicken, cold Christmas Pudding, malt whisky - that sort of stuff. There isn't water on mountaintops; each sleeper will need one litre overnight.

If it rains unexpectedly before bedtime, instead of the cold but splendid night you'll get a cold and miserable one. One warning: if you wake up cold and miserable you will want to skip breakfast in favour of getting moving, getting warm and getting down. Fine; but after no more than an hour, stop and eat. Not eating is bad. Another warning: don't bivvy down on a snowfield. There's been one involuntary descent of the Shelter Stone Crag by bivvy bag. It would be a shame to spoil that man's unique experience (he survived) by repeating it.

If you use the bivvy bag with premeditation night after night you must be a hill-runner. (in fact you're probably one of the five people known to me personally or else you are me.) The peculiar, very peculiar, joys of hill-running are in Chapter 6. The hill-runner's sack we peer into in Chapter 9. There we shall also empty out the big sack of the backpacker and weigh its contents.

Chapter 9

LUGGAGE

I find that 25lb is the most I can carry and still have fun and 30lbs is what I actually carry. On the Southern Upland Way we met a man who had on his back his entire supplies for a fortnight's walk. What a silly man - if he wants to go in for weightlifting why doesn't he do it in a gymnasium?

Here's the 30lb I carried on the Convenient Coast to Coast:

Item	weight		
	lbs	oz	Kg
Tent	4	0	1.8
Sleeping bag, Karrimat	4	6	2.0
Cooking gear	2	13	1.3
Spare clothes	5	0	2.3
Trainers	1	12	0.7
Fleece, waterproofs	2	8	1.1
Rucksack (empty)	3	12	1.7
Water (1 litre)	2	4	1.0
Food (4000 cal 1 day)	2	8	1.1
Emergency food	1	0	0.5
Total	29	15	13.5

Tent, cooker, sleeping bag, Karrimat
My sleeping bag is too heavy (3lb 12 oz). It is better to use a light bag and wear more inside it.

Spare clothes
Real savings in weight can be made here. Use several thin layers of modern, non-absorbent materials with a single skin waterproof or breathable outer shell. For the wealthy this means fleece and LIFA underwear: for the poor, acrylic, lycra, polyester, even old tights and bin liners. Avoid natural fibres like wool and cotton - they take forever to dry.

One of my best garments is a 100% acrylic polo-necked pullover that I found in the heather near Tom Buidhe (no you cannot have it back!) Lycra leggings are almost as warm and comfortable wet as dry; put them on under wet trousers for instant comfort. Women and extrovert men can also wear them in the pub.

Your dry sleepwear doubles as evening dress for the hotel and last-ditch blizzard-wear.

Trainers

Dry footwear for evening is essential for your feet. Trainers are heavy but I like them for road sections and always imagine I may want to run up the Corbett behind the bothy, though I never do.

Sundries

Maps, suntan cream, money, footpowder, aspirin, moleskin, piece of string. No book: paper and pencil and write a journal instead.

Water and Food

See next chapter.

Warm Hotel Walkers

The walker without the tent can also dispense with the cooker, Karrimat, sleeping bag and some spare clothes for night-time. It will now be possible to change down to a lighter 25 litre sack (empty sack weighs 2lb or 0.7kg).

The bivvi bag weighs 12 oz. The final weight ought to be below 20 lb which should allow fun and fast progress.

Runners

Here is the load I carried on a 2-day from Fife to the Clyde with a sub-zero bivouac on the Ochils....

Item	weight		
	lbs	kg	
Sleeping bag	2¼	1.0	
Bivvi bag	¾	0.4	
Spare clothes	4	1.8	(incl. fleece top, worn most of the way)
Camera	¾	0.3	(unnecessary)
4 Maps	1	0.5	
First aid etc.	½	0.2	
Sack empty	1½	0.7	
Food	4½	2.0	(8000 Cal, 1 1/2 days)
Water	2¼	1.0	(1ltr for initial urban section)
Total	17½	7.9	

130

FOOD AND GENERAL WELLBEING WITH SOME WORDS ON ENEMIES

Chapter 10

Food: Nutrition and Calories
Water
Foot Care
Miscellaneous Damage
Snow
Midges

FOOD

You think you get tired at the end of the day? You're wrong. Actually, you haven't had enough to eat. An eleven stone walker doing 10 to 12 hours a day needs 4000 Calories. The same person running would need 6000 Calories. Increase this if you weigh or walk more. Snickers bars come in at 500 Calories per 100 grams but not more than half your food should be fat or sugar. Most foods come in at 400 cal./100gm unless they contain moisture. Sandwiches contain moisture; so does dried fruit. Read the packaging for information.

As you get fitter you get hungrier. The lunch that sufficed on the first day will be too small a week later, even if you're walking the same distance. If your walking day has increased from seven hours to fourteen, you'll need at least two extra lunches.

Here are some raw data which you can cook up over your stove whatever way you like.

Protein	400 Cal/100gm
Carbohydrate	375
Fat	900
Alcohol	700
Fibre	0
Hot water	5

Protein: If you are getting enough Calories it is almost impossible not to get enough protein.

Sugar: The problem with carbohydrate in the form of sugar is that it hits the bloodstream very quickly giving a surge of energy followed by an upsurge ("going hypo" to diabetics, who know all about this). It is possible to use sugar as the mainstay of the diet but it should be taken in frequent small doses.

Complex Carbohydrate (CCH): These are the starch foods based on grains or potatoes. They are the preferred nourishment of the serious long-distance athletes because they release slowly into the bloodstream over a few hours.

Fat: It takes energy to digest fat and there may even be a small loss of vigour to start with. It is mobilised even slower than CCH: over half a day. It gives, though, nearly twice the food for the same weight and, as such, is very useful for backpackers, especially in the evening meal. Put butter in the evening cocoa like Scott of the Antarctic.

Your own body fat will be consumed more-or-less as if it were Mars bars: a pound of surplus bodyweight supplies 3500 Calories (770Cal/100gm).

Alcohol: Alcohol is a poison and it will decrease your next day's mileage. The effect is lessened if you supply your body with the means of flushing it out. Try drinking pints of beer and water alternately (starting with the water). A pint of beer does not contain enough water to flush out its own alcohol.

Hot Water: Hot food makes you feel good but as far as aiding survival goes you'd be better off eating the fuel blocks.

Fibre, vitamins and minerals: Because you're eating so much, you will probably get enough of these bits and pieces. Women walking or running to the limits of their endurance need to worry a bit about calcium and iron. (Make an effort to eat healthily at the hotel, where the food has been carried by lorry.) If your bowels aren't moving it's more likely to be dehydration.

The favourite foods of long-distance athletes have roughly equal quantities of fat and CCH, with a smaller quantity of sugar. (I've been unable to get a nutritional breakdown of Jos Naylor's wife's rock buns.)

CCH	oatmeal	410 cal/100gm	used by Bonnie Prince Charlie
	bread	250	contains moisture
	Smash Potato	410	
	Other dried potato	150	
Sugar	Plain sugar	370	
	Mars Bar	450	
	Snickers Bar	510	
	Dried Fruit	180-250	
Fat	Butter	800	
	Peanuts	600	
	Cheddar cheese	430	
Alcohol	Whisky	210	
Mixed	Sandwiches (honey)	330	Used by Eric Beard, and Martin Moran
	Christmas Pudding	370	Hugh Symonds
	Sweet biscuits	570	author's friend, Glyn
	Haggis	500	the author
	Complan	430	Ian Leighton

Water:

The Cuillin Ridge is waterless. Fifteen hours, we hope will be spent in brilliant sunshine. For this, 3 litres of water may be too little. In general, though, I carry a one-litre plastic bottle and I only fill it right to the top when the map shows a long dry stretch ahead.

It's worth noting that thirst comes when your body has too much salt for its water. Sweating, you lose water and salt together. You can get well dehydrated without any sensation of thirst. You can get dehydrated in the rain too. If you haven't had a pee for three hours, you're getting dehydrated.

Splashy and fast moving mountain streams contain oxygen which kills bacteria. Do not drink below inhabited buildings or sheepdips. Otherwise, unless there is a dead sheep immediately above, you are all right to drink. (A camper recently contracted liver-fluke on Arran. Liver-fluke lives in snails which live in slow-moving water with sheep.)

One litres of water weighs a kilogram. One pint weighs 1¼lbs.

FEET

The amount of fun you have depends more than anything else on how many blisters you get and how soon. When they're wet, your feet become soft and wrinkly like the underneath of a fish. Beat the underneath of a fish against a stone several thousand times and it will no longer be a useful surface for walking on.

* Try to minimise time spent on nasty hard roads. Steep rocky hillsides are much better for your feet.

* Wear the lightest most flexible boots you feel safe in regarding the terrain you intend to encounter. Wear them in beforehand: five full days in the rain should do it. If you carry trainers put them on, with dry socks, inside for the road sections.

* Buy a brand new pair of cushion-loop socks. If you're wealthy buy two pairs.

* Seize chances to get the wet out of your feet. First thing you do when you stop - dry socks. Lunch break? Take the feet out and wave them in the breeze. And before you put them back in, do what the Parachute Regiment does and powder them.

* Treat sore bits before they become blisters - with moleskin plasters or SPENCO.

* You've planned the route and measured it, you've weighed everything and put it into plastic bags, you've booked your accommodation and packed and unpacked your sack again three times: what's the one thing you forgot? You forgot to cut your toenails. Do it, or find them loose in your socks.

MISCELLANEOUS DAMAGE

Other Leg Injuries

It's hard for me to tell from up here in Scotland how bad your twisted ankle is. Maybe you've snapped off the bit of bone your ligament's fixed to. But maybe not. Injuries that hurt a lot or that don't get better in a few days should, of course, be seen by a doctor. Unless she's a runner herself, the doctor's going to say: "rest it!" Here are the things 1 try myself before limping off to the doctor. They work sometimes.

* **Cold water.** Dip the ankle, knee or other leg part in a stream. Keep dipping, for several minutes in each hour.

* **Ice.** Apply for several minutes. Ice should be wrapped in a spare undergarment, frozen peas left in their packet.

* **Aspirin/Iboprufen.** These are anti-inflammatories, acting to reduce swelling. They are also, as a side-effect, painkillers, so use them with discretion and bear in mind that if pain is killed, your brain rather than your nerve-endings now has responsibility for deciding how badly hurt you are.

* **Strapping, massage.** Strapping is elastic sticking plaster applied to compress the injured area and take some strain off damaged bits. Massage is pressing with thumbs until the patient goes "gosh, ouch!" Applied by an expert, such as a Chartered Physiotherapist, these can be very beneficial. Applied by an amateur, they probably won't make things any worse.

If you're lucky and the injury is on the mend, the following will help it on its way. Long term treatment is hot baths, twiddling your foot wherever it will go on the end of your leg and gentle exercise, to the point where it hurts just a little. Massage is good if you can get it. Complete rest is bad: it'll form scar tissue in the muscle.

Start-of-the-day exercises, as practised by the rare bird, the sensible hill-runner, put a bounce in your stride and prevent damage. Three minutes - while they're preparing your hotel bill - will do.

* Touch or attempt to touch your toes. (This stretches the hamstrings behind the knees, also the lower back)

* Heels on ground, attempt to push over a building or a tree. Hold. (Stretches backs of calves)

* Pick up the right toe in the right hand behind the right buttock. Hold. Then repeat with the left toe.. (Stretches fronts of thighs)

* Sit down. Wiggle feet on the ends of the legs everywhere they'll go. (Stretches the ankles)

Chafing: Wet underwear can chafe various precious bits. A smear of Vaseline is the answer.

Sunburn: Do not ignore this just because you are in Scotland. I have burnt on the hills far worse than on any beach.

Heatstroke: Heatstroke is dehydration, nothing else. The first symptom is tiredness, which may go unnoticed! Alarming is when you stop sweating because you have run out of water. A rapid rise in body-temperature, delirium and death follow. Treatment for advanced cases is to get the sufferer into the shade, or into a stream and give water. Treatment for the early stages is to drink water, often.

Exposure: Nowadays exposure is called hypothermia so that you can confuse it with hyperthermia, which is heatstroke. It is caused by being wet and cold, aggravated by being tired and underfed, and it leads to loss of judgment, which can twist back by way of :-

EXPOSURE → FUZZY BRAIN	getting lost ———→	MORE	wet
(wet, Cold,	bad route decision		cold
Tired, hungry)	bad decision to press on		tired
	bad decision not to eat		hungry

Apart from crossing old snow without an ice-axe, exposure is the commonest cause of death on our hills.

An early symptom of exposure is cold hands. This is dangerous in itself as it stops you from operating your zips and compass. Other signs to watch for are staggering, slurred speech, strange floaty feelings and obstinacy. These are easier to see in your companion than yourself; you'll say: "My shpeesh ish not schlurrd!"

Later and more dangerous signs are stopping shivering, inappropriate feelings of warmth and death.

If you are alert enough to spot the early rather than the late signs, just putting on more clothes will deal with it. Otherwise:-
* get out of the wind *now* rather than pressing forward in the hope of getting off the mountain eventually
* put on all clothing
* eat
* revise plans for the rest of the day

Exhaustion: If you feel exhausted, you should behave as if dying of exposure (see above); that is in fact what comes next. As you retreat from the hill, you may like to consider the following proposition. It isn't because you're tired. It's because:
* You haven't eaten enough
* You haven't drunk enough
* You are cold.

A car keeps going until it runs out of fuel and then stops: so why not a person? Well! your muscles are mot exactly the same as a car engine. All the same, if you want to cover more miles in a day try slowing down and eating more. As you get fitter you'll find to your surprise that if you keep on eating and drinking you can keep on walking until your feet get sore or night falls. Even odder: if you want, you can keep running.

SNOW

It's a little strange to include snow in a chapter on Enemies. Many of us will travel hundreds of miles for a day on a snow-covered Munro. Even for the axeless walker, a strip of moderately-old soggy snow gives a wonderful downhill run, especially if the alternative is some frightful boulder-slope.

Fresh snow isn't usually a problem unless it has fallen on steep, slippery grass and taken it just beyond the point of frighteningness. (You might like an axe even without the snow!) Old snow, which has thawed to slush and then frozen hard - perhaps several times, is more of a problem. If such a slope, which does not have to be steep, falls over a cliff or goes convex out of sight, keep off it unless you have an ice axe. Crossing old hard snow without an ice-axe is as sensible as crossing motorways blindfold.

The next bit of advice is like saying, "when crossing motorways blindfold, wear reflective clothing." However you might in some emergency be obliged to do one, in which case : -

* remove your windproof outer layer - on snow it's almost frictionless
* carry a pointed stone with which to attempt an ice-axe arrest
* cross one at a time. Often, when one person slides to their death, the others are so surprised they slide to their deaths as well.

MIDGES

A soldier at Glentrool in Galloway came close to being the first recorded case of death by midge bites. After an evening in the House o' Hill this unfortunate man got half undressed, got half way into his tent, and then collapsed in a stupor. When he was found in the morning his naked upper body was covered with midges - they had been eating his flesh all night.

The midges would have been female ones: the males do not bite. A midge spends most of her life as an underground maggot in the wet but not waterlogged ground that is rather common in the Western Highlands. She emerges into the air sometime between mid-May and mid-September, mates and then goes to look for two special meals. The first one, the carbohydrate one, consists of heather nectar if she's lucky and tree sap f she isn't. The second meal is you.

The midge is unusual among biting insects in being able to lay some eggs without her blood meal. With it, however, she can lay many more. (How many? They study midges only at Aberdeen and there's still a lot to find out.) As well as people she bites deer, sheep, rabbits and even birds. In Aberdeen they think man is her favourite. She sniffs you out (sweaty people are more attractive) and hunts you down at 2 mph.

You can go faster than that, so your first defence is to outrun her. So long as you keep walking she cannot catch you. Keep your stops short: the rate of arrival of midges at your skin surface increases in proportion to the time you have been standing.

Camp carefully. Once in Glen Cannich we camped in deep, wet bracken - it was dark and raining and we did not have much choice. In the morning the inside of the tent wall, formerly orange, was grey with midge. We struck camp with remarkable speed, rolling the tent up with vengeful tightness. We walked uphill and didn't stop for breakfast until we found a breeze. So if the air is still and the sky is midge grey, camp high where the grass is short and the breezes blow. Modern tents are midge proof, but when you put the tent up on the lawn before your trip, don't just count the pegs but also check the integrity of your midge defences.

You could also timetable to avoid midge hours around dawn and dusk. For instance you could lie in the tent until the sun is high and then walk until after dark.

Insect repellent cream is effective, especially the expensive brands - the midges only bite the places you missed. A natural plant-based alternative is Oil of Citronella, which has the added benefit of making you smell nice and the disadvantage, as we discovered in Glen Cannich, of not keeping off midges. Sticking your lower lip out and blowing across your face discourages them a bit. Mosquito coils, which you burn in the mouth of your tent, also work but fall to bits if carried for any distance in the rucksack.

The itch goes away after quarter of an hour - provide you do not scratch it. A well scratched midge-bite can last for days. Not scratching midge bites takes self-discipline and training, failing which there's antihistamine cream.

If you catch a midge feeding on your flesh, don't slap her - this spreads the midge-saliva further. Rub her to death gently with a fingertip. This is sport of a sort.

Chapter 11

PLANNING

Time and Distance
Maps
Foul Weather Alternatives: Control: Safety
Research
Access
Lochbui Forest: Routes Through an Imaginary Landscape

TIME & DISTANCE

There is no point in measuring distance without measuring climb. One thousand feet of ascent is as tiring as two extra miles, and takes as long as an extra one and a half miles. Part of your planning should be to measure the miles for each day - a piece of cotton is good enough for this - and count the contours. The time taken can be estimated with Naismith's Rule.

Naismith's Rule

Count each 1000 ft of ascent as an extra 1 1/2 miles (Each 400 metres as an extra 3 kilometres) Experience will give you your average speed but roughly:

2.5 mph (4kph)	Heavily laden walker
3 mph (5kph)	Fast, fit walker
4 mph (6kph)	Runner with bivvy bag
5 mph (4kph)	Runner, unladen

Speed, distance with 30lb will be about 2/3 normal.

To quickly (and accurately enough for most purposes) convert feet to metres multiply by 3 and knock off the 0. So 700 ft x 3 = 2100 then knock off the 0 = 210 metres. Actually the Munro level of 3000 ft is 914.4 metres not 900.

MAPS

1:250,000 Routemaster

These splendid maps - just two of them cover most of the Highlands - should be opened with care. Long-distance routes, including two in this book, spring out from between the folds. You can buy the maps flat in a roll to put on the wall but then you will spend a lot of time standing on a chair to look at them. Ideal for planning but you will need more detail for the actual walk.

1:50,000 Landranger

These superseded old one-inch maps we loved so dearly, ignoring their faults, which included misplaced paths and crags. Where a path appears on the

Landranger map, there is quite likely to be one in the real world and vice versa. On Sheet 33 the crag markings are so untidy that it looks as though it's been used to swat midges, which indeed it has. However the absence of such marks does often indicate a possible route. Where there's not just a path but a track marked, then there will really be one, though it may have nasty tarmac on. Blue "interesting to tourist" features are usually worth a wiggle in the route.

1:40,000 Harvey Maps
These maps, made for orienteers, are on waterproof paper and have lots of useful detail. They mark the rides through forestry plantations, which can save a lot of needles down the back of the neck. You probably won't buy them because they only do very interesting bits (Ben Lawers, Arrochar, Galloway) and you need the Landranger to get across onto the edge of the next Landranger.

1:25,000 Outdoor Leisure and Pathfinder
These have far more useful detail than you'll ever need to use. The Landranger does for everywhere except Skye and the Outdoor Leisure map of Skye has so many dead midge marks that it's impossible to see any of the useful detail. (Skye maps: see Chapter 2 afterword.)

FOUL WEATHER ALTERNATIVES: CONTROL: SAFETY

For each day that involves exposed mountain travel, you should also plan a foul weather alternative along a low sheltered route.

Control
Anyone on the hills should have left word of where they've gone and when they will be back. For a multi-day crossing you need more. You need a trust-worthy person on the phone with details of:-

* Your intended route and end-of-the-day stops (distance, climb)
* Your foul weather alternatives
* The extra things you will do if the heather-tang bites deeper than expected
* Where you will phone from and when
* How long after a missed phone call they summon the Rescue.
* Something about your competence and equipment (tents etc.) carried.

These details need to be in writing. TO CALL MOUNTAIN RESCUE PHONE THE POLICE (DIAL 999).
  A useful extra precaution for the lone walker is to record your passage in the visitors' books in bothies.

Walking Alone
Walking alone is more dangerous. It is also more fun, or anyway a different sort of fun. Within reason it's your decision how much risk to take for how

much fun. I walk alone often but I don't walk alone in Winter. People who cannot use a map and compass shouldn't walk alone, even in clear and settled weather.

I encourage experienced parties to carry extra copies of the map so that from time to time they can walk separately for half a day. It gives some unshared experience to talk about in the bothy.

Rescue

Mountain Rescue people are not paid (some of them are reimbursed for loss of earnings). Your rescue may involve ordinary climbers like me, most of whom will have just finished a day on the hill, most of whom will not even do anything heroic but just sit in a car at the bottom of the path waiting. These people will not mind too much that you are in difficulties through your own folly or ignorance. We are all ignorant fools from time to time. They will mind if you haven't made reasonable attempts to rescue yourself and they will mind very much indeed if you are discovered in the pub at closing time.

If you do get rescued, a contribution to the Mountain Rescue funds is appropriate - be very generous. Do not assume that you are going to be rescued, not in some of the country covered in this book. Before sliding into your bivvy bag and waiting for the helicopter, consider that they may take 24 hours to reach you: starting from when someone calls them out. It may be better to wait out the storm, eat lots of food and head on out.

Summary of Basic Safety
 * Leave word where you have gone
 * Carry a map and compass and know how to use them
 * Carry one more layer than you expect to wear
 * Carry 1/2 day more food than you expect to eat
 * Stay off snow or carry an ice-axe

RESEARCH

Bigger public libraries will have a full set of 1:50000 maps though they may be a bit out-of-date.

Tourist Information Centres issue useful, free leaflets with some of the available accommodation, places to see and transport details. The booklets also have nice pictures to stick into your route account. They will also send you photocopied bus timetables. I've given a lot of TI phone numbers: but any TI will give you the number of any other.

Your next recourse is to the yellow pages - again in your library. The headings you want are:

hotels and inns
guest houses and B&B
public houses
grocers and convenience stores
post offices

Post Offices? Well, if you want to find an inn near Alltdubh, look up Alltdubh post office which is Polvaird Bay 212. Now you look through the yellow pages for hotels with the Polvaird Bay exchange.

If your village shop is a crucial one, ring it up to find out when it closes and if it stocks butane cylinders (which it probably doesn't).

If the Yellow Pages fail you, then ring up the Tourist Information or the Post Office, explain why you want to know and ask.

The West Highland Way accommodation leaflet is useful where you cross it. Most of the bothies are listed in the MBA's maintenance list issued to members, with useful information on fuel supplies and when it was last mended. The books in the bibliography mention bothies too.

Eastern Escapes

A problem with any east Highland finish is that the last bit is actually low-lands. I give details of such routes as I know of: anyone who develops any off-road route out to the sea will perform a valuable service.

Spey Way: waymarked trail out to Spey Bay from Tomintoul by the Spey Valley. The variant from Loch Morlich is still under development.

West Gordon Way: 20 miles from east of Bennachie to Rhynie. Leaflet: Buchan Forest District, Portsoy Road, Huntley

Aberdeen: A former railway line is a walkway from Banchory to Aberdeen

Stonehaven: Dull forest roads can be followed to within a few miles of the town.

Arbroath: Abandoned railway nature trail covers only the last four miles.

ACCESS

Access to the upland areas of Scotland is free for all - well, fairly free. this is not, however, a right but a happy state of affairs. There are not as many of us here as in England or Wales; many landowners are hill people themselves. So far we've stayed on good terms for most of the time.

Simplified, the legal position is this: there is a law of trespass in Scotland and it says that the landowner may ask you to leave and may use reasonable force to evict you if you decline (so if you draw a tent-peg he may draw an ice-axe). He may bring a civil action against you for any actual damage you do and may shoot your dog in cold blood if he sees it, or think he sees it, chasing sheep. In practice you will have no access problems if you observe the points below. I have been turned off land twice in Wales but never in Scotland although I climb twenty Scottish hills for every Welsh one.

Enclosed Ground and Farmland
* Do not climb fences or stone walls: divert to the gate
* Close the gate
* Do not disturb livestock but walk quietly past beside the fence
* Do not leave litter
* Put your dog on a lead

Garbh Choire Mor from the South-east spur of Braeriach   *Photo: Jeremy Ashcroft*

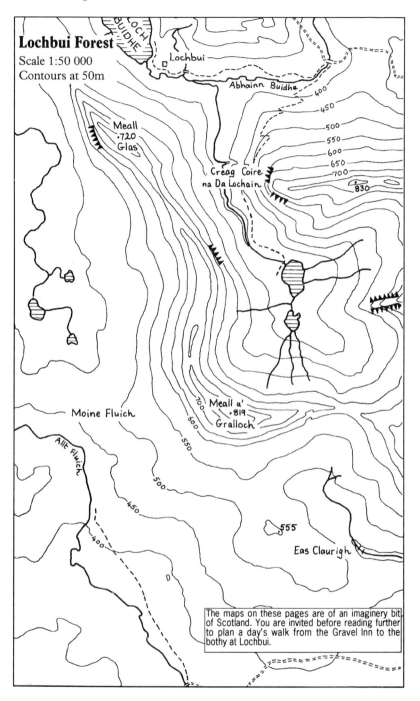

Lochbui Forest

Scale 1:50 000
Contours at 50m

Lochbui

Abhainn Buidhe

Meall
.720
Glas

Creag Coire
na Da Lochain

Moine Fluich

Meall a'
.819
Gralloch

Allt Fluich

555

Eas Claurigh

The maps on these pages are of an imaginery bit
of Scotland. You are invited before reading further
to plan a day's walk from the Gravel Inn to the
bothy at Lochbui.

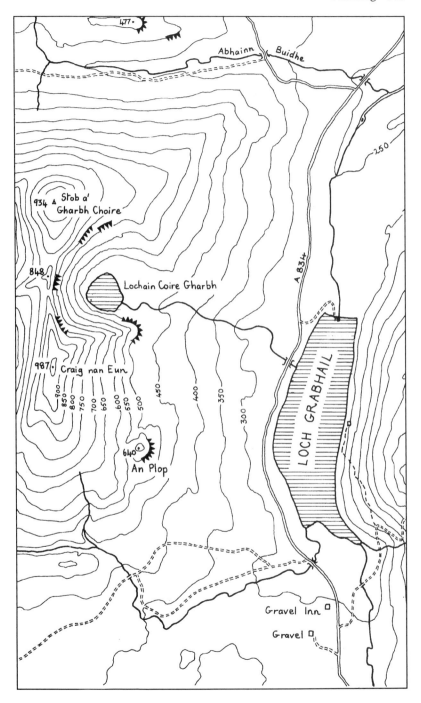

Lambing Time is the beginning of April to the end of May. Leave the dog at home and stay out of the fields with sheep in.

Moor and Mountain

* Grouse live on heathery moorland. During grouse nesting (again beginning of April to the end of May) walk, if possible, on tracks and paths and again restrict the poor old dog. On grass or rock, don't worry; grouse are not interested in grass.
* Grouse shooting season is from the 12th of August to 12th December (not Sundays). On an established route such as Glen Tilt, do not worry. On peaceful moorlands a phone call to the Factor's Office will save you from confrontations with armed men.
* Deer stalking starts around mid-August and continues until mid-October on most estates; then the killing of hinds, which is not a sport but work, may go on until mid February. Don't go unless you phone the factor's office first. Cameron McNeish's *Munroists Almanac* has a number to call for every Munro in Scotland: so does *Out & About in Scottish Hills* (SMT 1994).
* Glencoe, Torridon, Ben Lawers and the Galloway Hills belong to Us not Them and have no sporting restrictions.
* do not camp within ¼ of a mile of a house without asking(they'll almost certainly say yes).

Scotland doesn't have red lines on the map but we do have rights of way. Like other parts of Britain no-one knows if something is a right of way until it's been taken to court, which in general it hasn't. If you really need to know if it is a right of way phone the District Council (Planning Department or Leisure Services).

LOCHBUI FOREST: ROUTES THROUGH AN IMAGINARY LANDSCAPE

There are lots of right answers but here are some of the options worth considering.

* A834 and track beside Abhainn Buidhe and the other Abhainn Buidhe: a frightful route-choice. If the weather's that bad, better to spend a day in the bar.
* Monro's Tables reveal that we have two Munros here. Stob a' Choire Gharbh means "pointed peak of the rough corrie"; Craig nan Eun means "Crag of Birds". The Gaelic names suggest good peaks. The direct approach to Craig nan Eun from the south-east will be the choice of many, taking in the worthwhile small feature An Plop for the sake of its silly name. However, this shoulder is broad and uninteresting.
* Why not obey the Rule For Going Up Mountains and go *right into the corrie with the lochan in it* (Coire Garbh)? Well, because there's no

natural way into the Coire Garbh. Up stream bank (easiest way through the peat) to An Plop and then a tough moorland traverse: or seek a way round the east side of Loch Grabhail. Also, there's no easy way out of Coire Garbh. Well, that's the point. The slopes north-east of Craig nan Eun, though, don't look impossible. Where the thick (50m) contours are 2mm apart that's 27°; 27° feels like the side of a house but can usually be climbed. If, however, it can't be, then traverse south above the lowest crag onto the SE ridge, which is sharp but not too steep. Fill water bottles for the ridge while leaving the corrie.

★   The spur westward from point 848m to the two lochans looks serious. You'd have to be a confident scrambler indeed to embark on it, in descent, without prior knowledge of the difficulties. Consult the books in the Bibliography.

★   The ridge west of Stob a' Choire Gharbh looks interestingly narrow; perhaps it has frightful pinnacles? Again, consult the books.

★   The descent off Stob a' Choire Gharbh will be tricky in mist. One must descend NW for ten minutes to find the beginning of the interesting ridge, then west along it.

★   Off the unnamed top (830m), the ridge west has crag. Crag marks on maps don't necessarily mean much but this one has a Gaelic name so probably does exist: no descent here. The open slopes NW look fine; more interesting might be a descent SW to join the stalkers' path and pass under the ramparts of Craig na Da Lochain.

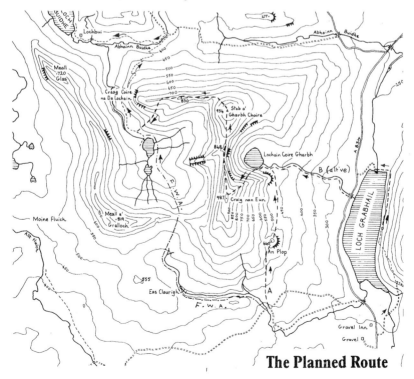

The Planned Route

Foul Weather Alternative: There's a fine high pass between Craig nan Eun and Meall Gralloch ("the hump of the disembowelling"). The approach to the pass is tough moorland; stay on the track westward as long as possible. Visit Eas Claurigh ("Roaring Fall"). The descent from the col is on a stalkers' path (note zig-zags) so should be comfortable. After rain don't head straight for the bothy but stay with the path to the footbridge.

★   If the foul weather becomes unexpectedly less foul, Meall Gralloch is a Corbett, though a dull one, and the ridge running north off it actually looks quite good. (But beware river crossing!)

★   Moine Fluich: wandering contours indicate boggy moor. Also, you won't be able to get across the river to the bothy. Bad FWA!

★   The whole day is a short one: 12 miles and 3000 ft - 7 hours at most. Load up heavily, then, for some serious bothy feasting to use up the end of the day, and consider carrying in fuel.

Author's suggested route:

Overnight Stop: Lochbui Bothy

Route Coire Garbh, Craig nan Eun, Stob a' Gharbh Choire

Foul Weather Alternative: Col Meall Gralloch/ Craig nan Eun (possible diversion over Meall Gralloch)

Chapter 12
REFERENCE

History
Getting to Grips with Gaelic
Book List
Useful Addresses

HISTORY

From the dawn of civilisation, the fundamental economic activity of the Highlands (and of the Southern Uplands equally) was stealing cattle. The comings and goings of enthusiastic cattle-thieves are naturally unrecorded but many a respectable drover from Argyll or Skye must have fancied the prices at Perth against the more convenient Falkirk or Stirling and driven them coast-to-coast. Earlier still, business travel between his two foundations will have taken St Aidan on foot between Lindisfarne and Iona. (To repeat his journey refer to the booklist for Not the SU Way in Chapter 5: the West Highland Way and the beginning of Summits of the South then get you to Oban for the Mull ferry.)

So far the only Royal crossing has been that of Prince Charles Edward Stewart between May and September of 1746. His route was long, complicated and interesting, starting at Culloden near Inverness and taking in Craig Meagaidh, Ben Alder, Lochaber (twice), Glen Affric and Skye. You can see the compass he used at Dunvegan Castle: it's made of ivory. High-ranking readers may note, though, that the record for the fastest Royal crossing remains wide open.

The first munroists, Naismith, Robertson and Munro himself, walked for days on end: many of their expeditions ended on the West Coast. If none of them started on the eastern one, that's only because they were more interested in climbing hills than crossing maps.

In their day travel was slow and difficult, even where there were roads and the shepherds' cottages many of them our present day bothies) were still inhabited and offered warmth, food and shelter.

During the middle part of the century roads crawled into many - too many - of the glens and the attention of serious mountaineers turned to serious mountaineering and away from peak-bagging. Peak-baggers did so using their cars as a base while hiking was done by earnest young people in long shorts between Youth Hostels. The existence of Glen Affric Youth Hostel suggests that a few of these, too, will have completed and enjoyed their coast-to-coasts.

However it is the development of the lightweight tent that has made coast to coasting an undertaking not simply possible but enjoyably possible for any reasonably fit person. The first outdoor challenge (at that time called the

Ultimate Challenge) was in 1979. Since then at least two hundred people have coast to coasted each year.

The first "fast and high" crossing was by Robin Harris and Ian Leighton in 1983: they ran from Inverie (Knoydart) to Montrose in four and a half days. It would have been a little less but for an impulsive decision on the Lochnagar Plateau to divert to Ballater for chips. They crossed 18 Munros, including all the 4000 foot ones, the Grey Corries, Lochnagar and Mount Keen. To avoid carrying warm clothing for nighttime they planned to sleep only during the day and they subsisted on Complan and glucose.

In 1985 they went back to cover some of the hills they had left out. This time they crossed from Shiel Bridge to Montrose, covering 280 miles, 80,000 feet and 42 Munros in 6 days. The Munros were the South Cluanie Ridge (9), Ben Nevis to the Grey Corries (8), Loch Ossian (5), the Ben Alder group (9), the Cairngorms (10) and Mount Keen.

Good snow cover rarely extends to Montrose, so Balmoral is the starting point for the Scottish *Haute Route*. This high level ski-mountaineering trip was undertaken by Mike Taylor and David Grieve in February 1978. They took 7 days to cover 99 miles, experiencing wet blizzards on moors east of Dalwhinnie and crossing 8 Munros and a Corbett (the Fara).

A full coast to coast was achieved in January 1982 on Nordic (cross-country) skis: admittedly a short one, from Loch Duich to Beauly, but in an extraordinary time of 17 hours. The team was Sam Crymble, Keith Geddes, Tim Walker and Blyth Wright, all from Glenmore Lodge. They made particularly good time across the frozen lochs of Glen Affric.

GETTING TO GRIPS WITH GAELIC

The Gaelic Language is as deep as a mountain stream, full of strange turnings and sudden falls, and with an uncomfortable rocky bottom. Here am I splashing around in it saying, "It's not too cold at all once your in!" Now the one you really want to talk to about this is a primary school child from Wester Ross, but, if you don't know any, here's enough to get you started.

1   Stress the first syllable (assuming you can find it).
2   Pronounce as many vowels as you can.

So we have Sgurr nan Each (Peak of the Horses) "SKURR nan EE-ach" with the "ch" as in Scots "Loch". Gaelic is not pronounced gaylick but "GAH-elick", somewhere between "Gallic" and "Garlic".

Now for the consonants:
3   Consonants not followed by H are pronounced approximately as in English..
4   ...except that S, T before or after E or I (the "small vowels") are pronounced "SH", "TH".
An Teallach (the Forge): "An CHAY-lach"
Seanna Bhraigh (Old Hillside) "SHEE-ana VRAY"

5   C is always hard like "K", never soft like "S".
Bealach na Lice (Pass of the Rock Slabs) "BAY-alach na LEE-kah".
Rule 2a You always pronounce the final E.

6   When a noun goes into the Genetive, an adjective into the female
form, its first consonant adds H and changes its sound in weird ways.
Muileann (Mill) "MOO-lin" same word as in French.
Allt a' Mhuilinn (Stream of the Mill) "Alt a VOO-lin".
Beinn (mountain) "Ben". more accurately "BUY-in".
Ladhar Bheinn (Filth Hill) "LAR-ven".

7   BH is pronounced "V" at the beginning or end of a word, silent
elsewhere.
MH is pronounced "V" at the beginning of a word, silent elsewhere.
DH and FH are silent.
GH is a gutteral noise but silence may be best for beginners.
Beinn Mheadhoin (Middle Hill) "Ben Vane"
Carn an Fhidhleir (Fiddler's Heap) "CAR-nan YEEL-ah"

8   TH is pronounced "H" at the beginning of a word, silent elsewhere.
Sgurr Thormaid (Norman's Peak) "SKURR HORR-madj"

9   In the formation AN-T-S, the S is silent.
Meall an-t-Suidhe (Hump of the Seat) "Melantee"

When you climb a hill you like, look it up in the excellent glossary in *Munro's Tables* or *Scrambles in Skye*. The rules above will help you understand why it's pronounced the way they say and you will gradually build up a vocabulary. I give you below just two lists to start you off: words meaning hill and colours.

Words for Hill

Sgurr	rocky peak
Stob	a spike
Creag	crag
Beinn	mountain
Stac	Sticky-up bit
Cruach	Stack-shaped hill (steep-sided)
Aonach	Ridge, long narrow hill
Mam	Breast-shaped hill
Sail	Heel-shaped hill
Sron	Nose-shaped hill
Carn	Heap of stones (from 2ft to 4000 ft)
Meall	Hump (a dull hill)
Monadh "Mona"	Moor, high plateau
Cnap	Knob
Cnoc	Small hill.

Colours

Dearg "JERR-ack"	reddish grey
Ruadh "RUE-a"	reddish brown
Odhar "OH-ar"	pale brown
Uaine "YOO-inner"	green
Gorm	blue-green
Liath "LEE-a"	blue-grey
Glas	greenish-grey
Dubh "DOO"	Black
Geal	white, brownish white
Ban	white, greyish white, quartzite colour
Fionn	white, fair
Riabhach "REE-avach"	mottled

BOOK LIST

Crossings of Scotland
The Great Walking Adventure: Hamish Brown (Oxford Illustrated Press)
  Scotland Coast-to-Coast: Hamish Brown (Patrick Stevens Ltd)
  A detailed guidebook for a low level route from Shiel Bridge to Arbroath.
Macgregor Across Scotland (BBC 1991)
  Not a detailed guide but pleasant gossip and photos on a low level route
  from Montrose to Ardnamurchan.
For the Southern Upland Way see Chapter 5.

General Guide Books
West Highland Walks:
  One (Ben Lui to the Falls of Glomach)
  Two (Skye to Cape Wrath)
  Three (Arran to Ben Lui)
Highland Walks:
  Four (Cairngorms & Deeside)
  All by Hamish MacInnes on Hodder & Stoughton. Very useful and
  about 1000 miles per volume.
100 Best Routes on Scottish Mountains: Ralph Storer (David & Charles - hard-
back; Sphere -paperback)
  Storer's idea of a good route often involves scrambling, and this is the
  place to find out just how interesting that interesting ridge is going to be.
The Munros (SMC District Guide) covers all the Munros, so useful for
  warning you off the dull ones.
The High Mountains of Britain and Ireland Vol. 1: Irvine Butterfield (Diadem)
  High mountains means over 3000 feet, which is hard on England and
  Wales. Another complete guide to the Munros with over 200 inspiring
  colour photographs but I find Storer more exciting. Volume 2 is due for
  publication in 1994/5 by Ken Wilson's new BatonWicks imprint. It will
  cover the Corbetts and their English, Welsh and Irish equivalents.

The Corbetts and other Scottish Hills: (SMC District Guide)
For the discriminating - not a Munro in it.
Classic Walks in Scotland: Cameron McNeish and Roger Smith (Oxford IllustratedPress)
Bridge of Orchy - Dalmally; Glenfinnan - Tomdoun; Dalwhinnie - Fort William; Braemar -Stonehaven and Corrieyairack plus about 400 miles of shorter walks in circles.
The Waterfalls of Scotland: Louis Stott (Aberdeen University Press)
A very thorough guide. A couple of these waterfalls will greatly improve your route.

Inspirational
Mountaineering In Scotland/Undiscovered Scotland: WH Murray (now published in one volume by Diadem)
Great adventures, lovely writing. This one could turn you from a backpacker to a mountaineer.
Scottish Mountain Climbs: Donald Bennett (Batsford)
Some climbs on paths, some on snow and ice; with glossy photos.
Hamish's Mountain Walk: Hamish Brown (Gollancz)
The first continuous walk over all the Munros. HB has done them so often now that it takes a book for the dull bits.
The Munros in Winter: Martin Moran (David & Charles)... but doing them all in Winter makes a more exciting read.

General
Mountaincraft and Leadership: Eric Langmuir (Scottish Sports Council)
May save you from getting killed while amassing the necessary experience to cross Scottish hills safely.
Scotland's Winter Mountains: Martin Moran (David & Charles)
Equal parts inspiration and instruction. Why spend Winter waiting for Summer?
Midges in Scotland: George Hendry (James Thin the Mercat Press)
Know your enemy!

USEFUL ADDRESSES

Walkers and Runners
Long Distance Walkers Association:
Sec: Brian Smith 10 Temple Park Close, Leeds LS15 0JJ Tel 01532 642205
Membership Sec: Geoff Saunders, 117 Higher Lane, Rainford, St. Helens, Merseyside WA11 8BQ Tel. 01744 882638

Scottish Hill Runners' Association
Sec: Robin Morris, 33 Morningside Road, Edinburgh EH10 4DR Tel 0131 447 8846
Membership: Andy Curtis, 35 Aquila drive, Heddon on the Wall, Northumberland.

Fell Runners' Association
  Sec: Mike Rose, 15 New Park View, Farsley, Leeds LS28 5TZ Tel 01532 556603
  Membership: Pete Bland Sports, 34a Kirkland, Kendal, Cumbria LA9 5AD Tel 01539 731012

Events
The Great Outdoor Challenge
  Roger Smith, The Great Outdoors, The Plaza Tower, East Kilbride, Glasgow G74 1LW Entry form is in the November issue of *The Great Outdoors* magazine.

Karrimor International Mountain Marathon (sometimes in England or Wales)
  Jen Longbottom, Karrimor, Petre Road, Clayton-le-Moors, Accrington, Lancs BB5 5JP. Tel 01254 398531

Rohan (Rock + Run) Mountain Marathon
  Rohan, 30 Maryland Road, Tongwell, Milton Keynes, MK15 8HN. Tel 01908 618888

Rings of Fire (Galloway 50 Mile)
  Glyn Jones, Bing, Kirkinner, Wigtownshire DG8 9BZ

Other Addresses
Scottish Youth Hostels Association
  7 Glebe Cresecent, Stirling, FK8 2JA (or join at any hostel)

Ramblers' Association, Scotland
  Crusader House, Balgonie Road, Haig Business Park, Markinch, Fife KY7 7AQ Tel 01592 611177

Mountain Bothies Association
Information Sec: Ted Butcher, 26, Rycroft Avenue, Deeping St James, Peterborough, PE6   8NT Tel. 01778 345062

Scottish Rights of Way Society
  1 Lutton Place, Edinburgh, EH8 9PD

Scottish Landowners' Federation
  18 Abercrombie Place, Edinburgh EH10 5JR

Highland Guides
  Inverdruie, Aviemore, Invernessshire PH22 1QH Tel 01479 810729

NOTES

NOTES

NOTES

NOTES

NOTES

....
....
....
....
....
....
....
....
....
....
....
....
....
....
....
....
....
....
....
....
....
....
....
....
....
....
....
....
....
....
....
....
....
....
....

NOTES

Other Outdoor Guides from Grey Stone Books

The Welsh Three Thousands by Roy Clayton
An invaluable guide for walkers, fellrunners, backpackers and youth hostellers for the 27 mile traverse of Wales 3000 feet summits. Also included are the various ascents of Snowdon, the Snowdon Horseshoe Walk and the Welsh 1000 Metre race. Harvey Lloyd, warden of the Pen-y-Pass Youth Hostel gives a fascinating account of the history of the Three Thousands event, including the best times. Illustrated with black and white photos and John Gillham's 3D maps and line drawings
Paperback 80 pages 124mm x 186mm   £4.50

Peaks of the Yorkshire Dales by John Gillham & Phil Iddon
A popular book which describes 31 mainly circular walks to the highest peaks in the Yorkshire Dales.The celebrated mountains of Ingleborough and Pen-y-Ghent are featured alongside lesser-known summits such as Great Coum above Dent and Rye Loaf Hill above Settle. There are 18 full-page colour photos and the maps are 3D panoramas.
Paperback: 128 pages 210 x 148   £8.95

Bowland & The South Pennines by John Gillham
This is a celebration of some of England"s wildest uplands - all within reach of the towns and cities of Lancashire, Yorkshire and Greater Manchester. John Gillham describes 33 walks - some to Bowland's - heather moors and some to the lofty gritstone-capped summits of the South Pennines. Phil Iddon describes routes to Pendle Hill, which lies sandwiched between the two ranges. There are 12 full-page colour photos and many black and white photos - the maps are 3D panoramas.
Hardback 122 pages 210 x 148   £9.95

The Bowland Dales Traverse by John Gillham
The Bowland-Dales Traverse is a long-distance route spanning 85 miles between Garstang near Preston to Richmond in Yorkshire, threading through some of the loveliest hill country of the Forest of Bowland and the Yorkshire Dales. Visited en route are the heather-clad Calder, Brennand and Dunsop fells, Slaidburn, Settle, Malham, Kettlewell, Buckden Pike, the Aysgarth Falls, Castle Bolton and Reeth. The pocket book is illustrated by line drawings and black &white photos.
Hardback 64 pages 105 x 148   £2.95

All the books should be available at your local bookstore. In the case of any difficulty they can also be ordered post-free from Cordee 3a DeMontfort Street, Leicester LE1 7HD. Prices correct at time of printing (1994) and are based on the present zero rate of VAT .